"Part of my role includes being an exp
able energy projects, so I know how
and words are. In his book Mark m
and strings these together in a uniqu
changing way. Perhaps the most powerful connection .. ....
that our words and thoughts give rise to our feelings, and combining that with the effective strategies for conversation gives us a
simply written, totally empowering and hugely inspiring book."
Sitara Keppie, Managing Director, Circle Design (UK) Ltd

"We live in a world where both in our personal and business lives
electronic communication has become the norm. It has been said that
many people are actually losing the skill of simply talking to people.
In this book, Mark Rhodes, in his easy-to-read down-to-earth style,
gives all of us a solid framework to maximize our effectiveness in
starting conversations in any situation naturally. In doing so he ensures
we will achieve the outcomes we want. Thoroughly recommended."
Robbie Stepney, Managing Director, Calls That Count Limited

"*How to Talk to Absolutely Anyone* goes way beyond the promise
made in the title. An enlightening mixture of common sense and
practical experience that is both extremely readable and imple-
mentable. Mark has brought to the book the same style that makes
him such a great speaker at live events. The ideas for how to
approach difficult conversations are a huge bonus, changing the
focus to a win–win mindset."
Ray Noble, Editor, *Your Excellency* **Magazine www.yourexcel
lencymag.com**

"In business, as in all walks of life, communication is vital whatever
we are doing. Yet how often do we think about how to engage
with others in the best way or how to enhance our skill set in this
area? Mark, in his clear and engaging way, gives readers the opportunity to overcome their in-built fears, practice and improve their
skills and learn new ones. Personally, I have learnt a great deal
from Mark and have valued reading this book."
Peter Quilt

"This book shows you how to make your thinking work for you – not against you – so that you can talk successfully with anyone, anywhere. As has been said of Mark's previous book (on success) – keep it with you and read it over and over again!"
Mark Henry, Corporate and Banking Partner, Birketts LLP

"I have seen so many intelligent people held back by their weak communication skills, their fear of 'speaking to strangers' in a business environment. It is one thing to tell them they are needlessly being held back; what this book does is detail the practical route to overcoming these fears and being a better communicator – a kind of 'sat-nav for stress-free mingling'!"
Danny Clifford, Managing Partner, Ensors

"As the world's largest Business Networking organization we know that communication, and the ability to be able to build relationships, are absolutely crucial for business and personal success. Mark has been the headline speaker for a number of our conferences and now brings his knowledge and experience in the area of communication to everyone in *How to Talk to Absolutely Anyone*."
Charlie Lawson, National Director, BNI UK & Ireland

"Whatever age, background or stage of life you are at, Mark's positive voice of experience connects with you to deliver a myriad of real-life situations and solutions so you can develop the know-how to get the best out of communication, and get the best out of life!"
Siobhan Eke, Director of Enterprise and Innovation Principalship, City College Norwich

How to Talk to Absolutely Anyone

Confident communication for work,
life and relationships

SECOND EDITION

Mark Rhodes

CAPSTONE
A Wiley Brand

Registered office

Capstone Publishing Ltd. (A Wiley Company), John Wiley and Sons Ltd, The Atrium, Southern Gate, Chichester, West Sussex, PO19 8SQ, United Kingdom

For details of our global editorial offices, for customer services and for information about how to apply for permission to reuse the copyright material in this book please see our website at www.wiley.com.

The right of the author to be identified as the author of this work has been asserted in accordance with the Copyright, Designs and Patents Act 1988.

Library of Congress Cataloging-in-Publication Data

Names: Rhodes, Mark, 1966- author.
Title: How to talk to absolutely anyone : confident communication for work, life and relationships / Mark Rhodes.
Description: Chichester, West Sussex, United Kingdom : John Wiley and Sons, [2017] | Includes index. |
Identifiers: LCCN 2017020142 (print) | LCCN 2017029761 (ebook) | ISBN 9780857087485 (pdf) | ISBN 9780857087478 (epub) | ISBN 9780857087454 (pbk.)
Subjects: LCSH: Interpersonal communication. | Self-confidence. | Attitude (Psychology)
Classification: LCC HM1166 (ebook) | LCC HM1166 .R46 2017 (print) | DDC 155.2—dc23
LC record available at https://lccn.loc.gov/2017020142

Cover design adapted from the first edition design by Revert to Type; used with permission

Set in 11.5/15pt Adobe Caslon Pro-Regular by SPi Global, Chennai, India

They say that everyone needs a mentor. Whenever I heard this I thought – yes, except me! I always believed I didn't need a mentor. I was able to leverage other materials such as books, DVDs and my own thoughts to mentor myself.

However, quite recently I realized the reason I didn't need a mentor was because I already had one!

All this time I had a mentor; who gave me encouragement when I had doubts and positivity whenever I felt negative about something.

My mentor even helped me by believing in me when the going got tough and was also quick to remind me on a regular basis of all the achievements I had made.

In addition to my mentor I also have two motivators who inspire me to do and be more.

Therefore, this book is dedicated with love to my mentor and wife Jackie Rhodes, and, of course, to my two motivators and inspirers – our children Holly and James.

Contents

In memory of Fred

About the Author

Author photo by Peter Evans Photography (www.peterevansphoto.com)

Mark Rhodes is an entrepreneur, mentor, international speaker and trainer in success who shows people how to massively improve their results with little or no extra effort! He is also the author of *Think Your Way to Success*, published in 2012 by Wiley.

Mark empowers individuals in their lives, careers and businesses. He has also "been there and done it" – from the ground up, he started, built and ran his own Internet software company, which he then sold to a USA Silicon Valley organization in 2001. This was just two years after starting the business in 1999. Mark's clients included top brand names such as The Body Shop at home, Virgin Cosmetics and Dorling Kindersley Publishers.

On selling his company, Mark retired at the age of 35, but only for fifteen minutes before he got bored!

Mark was keen to figure out how he had become successful and now spends his time teaching others, so that they can achieve their own dreams. Mark's focus is on what he believes to be one of the most crucial aspects of whether someone achieves success or not, their "success mindset", as well as the business-specific topics of "winning more sales" and "exceeding goals" – because of the simple fact that most people don't set a big enough goal! In everything Mark does and teaches, communication and the words we use are paramount.

In addition to speaking at conferences and events, Mark is a trainer and mentor for people who want to succeed. Mark makes everything so easy to understand and implement. His natural, down-to-earth style and the fact that he teaches the exact same tools and techniques that he uses every day in his own life is a refreshing change.

Mark speaks internationally for many types of businesses at both conferences and internal staff development events. For more information, go to Mark's website at www.markrhodes.com where you can find out about his speaking engagements and sign up for his free content of video, audio and articles to support this book and your success in general. You'll also find out about events where Mark is speaking live and details of his online webinars.

There are also details on the website about Mark as a speaker and mentor around the world and how to get in touch with him.

Foreword by Armand Beasley

I have to admit that I was slightly puzzled and taken aback when Mark approached me to write the Foreword for *How To Talk To Absolutely Anyone*. You see, my forté is makeup, beauty, grooming and style. So I was a bit confused as to why Mark would approach me to write a foreword for this kind of book. But then I thought about it and as soon as I started to read it everything clicked into place!

As a makeup artist and beauty/image expert I have been fortunate to work with some of the most beautiful and successful men and women in the world. Individuals who appear to exude confidence whether they are on the red carpet or performing on a stage in front of thousands!

Yet for years I have been a regular face on British TV makeover shows, giving advice and transforming the Great British Public from "drab" to fab. The appetite for these types of shows is relentless . . . People WANT to make the most out of themselves. It doesn't have to cost the earth or take a huge amount of time and effort. Indeed looking and feeling fabulous is NOT just for the rich and famous . . . it's an achievable goal that can work into everyone's timeframe and budget!

The main attribute you need is not Angelina Jolie's perfect pout, or Hugh Jackman's six pack – it's confidence!

Identifying and highlighting your best features will set you on the road to a renewed confidence in yourself.

How To Talk To Absolutely Anyone gives you easy-to-follow steps and ideas on how to instantly boost your confidence to approach anyone in any situation. From tackling sensitive work-related issues to breaking the painfully awkward silence of "lift" travel, this book is an easily digestible read that helps to rethink your approach to socially and personally challenging situations.

I think this is the perfect travel companion as it is easy to skim through to areas of concern for you, as well as containing handy confidence-boosting techniques for so many tricky situations.

This book really helps you to move your comfort zone, in a similar way that a red lipstick can for a woman or a skin-care routine can for a man. There's that classic Fear Factor: "there's no way I can say that!", "there's no way I can wear that . . . ", but Mark's refreshing approach on addressing real-life situations will have an instant effect on how you interact with friends, family and total strangers. After years of public speaking and hosting various events, even I have picked up some invaluable tips.

Like Mark's sellout seminars, his sense of fun and enthusiasm exudes throughout the book, allowing you to relate to the various scenarios regardless of your background.

Enjoy!

Armand

Armand Beasley

International beauty/image expert and celebrity makeup artist

www.armandinternationalltd.com

Introduction: Why You Should Want to Talk to Absolutely Anyone

Communication, the ability to talk to other people, is one of the most important skills you can develop in life. We communicate with other people all of the time. Sometimes it's easy, but at other times it can seem impossible.

This book will give you the tools to become a more natural and effective communicator. You'll become better at talking to people you already know and discover what it is that stops you interacting with people you don't. By the end, you'll be communicating more confidently and more often, and your communication will be sharper; giving you a better chance of getting the outcomes you're looking for, more often.

Part One covers the fears associated with starting conversations, from the fear of rejection to worries about what other people might think. You'll also find out how you can reverse the negative feelings that are inbuilt in most of us about communicating with strangers.

Part Two is a walkthrough of the four main stages of an interaction. You'll learn lots of new skills to help you get more of what you want from a conversation or communication, including how to identify who to talk to and who not to talk to, how to open the conversation, how to get people interested in what you've got to say, and how to lead them in the general direction you'd like the conversation to go.

Part Three is a master class in making your communication even better, by working on voice and other conversation techniques. It also covers common pitfalls and you'll learn how to deal with difficult conversations such as telling someone they've made a mistake or asking somebody to do something for you.

Of course, armed with all this information you need to take action, get out there and start talking to people. That's where the daily development plan comes into play at the end of the book. This plan gives you a day-by-day process to start really easily, and then gradually build up your skills and confidence. Then you'll be able to talk to absolutely anyone – if you want to that is!

Communication Is All About Understanding

The person you're talking to needs to feel that you understand them and, of course, they need to understand you as well. It is only when you reach a place of mutual understanding that real progress can be made and rapport can grow.

There are two main levels of communication:

1. Primary communication – the actual words you say and the direct meaning that somebody gets from those words.
2. Secondary communication – when people assume or deduce something that you didn't intend from what you say.

Secondary communication is what happens outside the actual words you say – from the impression you create to the multiple interpretations your words are open to.

Let's say you tell somebody that you're paying for a friend to go on holiday. You may assume that they'll think you're a generous person, but the real secondary communication might be that the listener gains a negative impression of your friends. They may think you have friends who survive on handouts: not at all what you intended your communication to achieve.

Many communication problems come back to the "communication gap"; the difference between what you mean when you say something to someone and **the meaning they take away**.

So why would this be any different? Why would there be a communication gap? Language is really the expression of how you feel about something. Emotions are generated when you have thoughts or experience things in the outside world. You then put together words to express those emotions and say what it is you want, think or need, etc. This all happens at a subconscious level, without the need to think about every word you are going to say.

The gap comes about because different people use different phrases and words to explain their internal or emotional experiences. When you describe something to another person using specific words and phrases, those words and phrases might be different from how they themselves would describe that exact same experience. That means that no one else is likely to fully experience or process the language you use in exactly the same way as you.

Add to this the fact that no one thinks exactly like you do. We've all had different experiences and see the world and our place in it differently. We have varying beliefs and values. Your communication is based upon things that *have* happened, things that *are* happening or things that you *want* to happen in life. There is always internal processing and it is this that varies from person to person.

Imagine a car pulls out in front of you when you are driving down the road. Before you say anything to your passenger, your mind processes the event by considering:

→ Your values – what you consider important in life.
→ Your beliefs – what you believe people should and shouldn't do when driving and how people should and shouldn't treat each other.
→ Your previous experiences of driving and similar situations.
→ Your assumptions and expectations or thinking about what could have happened in that situation.

After processing all of this on a subconscious level, there are a range of possible comments you may make to your passenger in response.

Possible Positive Responses	Possible Negative Responses
They are a careless driver.	They had no regard for my safety.
They didn't see me.	How dare they do that to me!
They must have something really urgent to get to.	They are obviously a horrible person.

Your reaction will probably be different to theirs had they been driving. The same external event produces a different response with different language attached to it.

Words mean different things to different people and vary in different situations.

If I say "I've had a fantastic holiday", for example, that doesn't necessarily mean you'll have a fantastic holiday too, just by going to the same place and doing the same things as me. You will have an entirely different set of criteria for what constitutes "fantastic" in respect of a holiday. Likewise, think about the word *outspoken*. For some people it's a compliment, implying frankness and honesty. For others, it implies criticism.

It's all about how you process different experiences. Your experiences cause you to use certain words and phrases but you can never be sure that the person you are talking to shares your experiences. That's why there is always a communication gap.

We Notice Different Things

Why is it that two people can witness the same event but come up with completely different interpretations? According to Neuro Linguistic Programming (NLP), when you experience something in the outside world, your mind selectively siphons down the information it is bombarded with, to between five and nine things that it can pay attention to at any one time. The things you siphon off will be different to those that other people do.

We tend to notice the things that are most relevant to us or reflect our worldview. That's why two people can go to the same event and have a very different experience: they notice different things in the same environment. Let's say Person A is scared to be at a football match because there may be tension in the crowd. Due to his preconceptions about the event, he is more likely to notice people who are frowning. Person B goes to the same match expecting people to be relaxed and friendly. He is more likely to notice smiles and laughter. The same event, but a completely different experience.

If you've ever bought a car, you may have had this experience. After you select the make, model and colour you want, you'll rarely, if ever, see that exact car on the road. Your brain doesn't think that things you *want* are relevant to you.

When you eventually get the car though, you start to see similar ones everywhere! Either the universe has decided to put a load more out there just to frustrate you or they were always there and you just weren't seeing them. So what has changed? Now that you've got the car your mind sees similar ones as highly relevant, so they show up in the "five to nine things" your consciousness is currently processing.

We are all unique. We see the world differently even when presented with the same external stimulus. No wonder so many of us feel unsure about starting conversations. Communication is a minefield, but your future opportunities, success and happiness depend on your interaction with other people – and that's where this book comes in.

You can use the content to develop your communication skills in all sorts of situations, whether you want to expand your social life, be that confident person who can strike up a conversation with anyone, or get better at selling or networking. Whatever it is, you'll find strategies, ideas and techniques in this book to help you talk to absolutely anyone!

PART ONE

Common Fears and Barriers about Talking to Absolutely Anyone

1
Fear – Does It Hold You Back?

Like most people, you'll have experienced situations where you've held back from saying certain things or starting conversations. It can happen with people you know well and with people you don't. Some of this is due to a lack of skillset – simply not knowing how to start or handle a conversation. But there's another factor that holds many people back and that's fear. Perhaps you don't label it "fear". Perhaps you call it "uncertainty", or maybe you pass the moment off because it "just doesn't seem right". However you justify it though, it is one or another form of fear that is presenting itself and stopping you.

It could be the worry about what other people might think. It may be concern about looking stupid or making a mistake. Or it could be fear of rejection. After all, you're not holding back because you're worried people will accept you with open arms, are you?

So what is fear and what can you do to change the "fear feeling" and get to a point where you're comfortable taking action?

Fear is an emotional reaction to a situation you are in or thinking about. Your thoughts about the situation dictate how you feel or the emotions you experience, and that determines the action you take (or don't take). In turn, the quality of the action you take determines the result you get, which feeds back into the thoughts you associate with the situation in future.

For example, you're likely to feel good about a meeting if you're excited about the information you're going to share. Enthusiasm means you are likely to perform very well and get a good result. Next time a similar meeting comes up you're going to be very positive about it because of past results.

Of course the same is true of the things you fear. When you think about something going badly you don't feel great about the situation and are unlikely to perform to the best of your abilities.

Remember this important formula:

Thoughts → Feelings → Action → Results

What Exactly *Is* Fear?

Fear is your emotional response to a situation that is happening or that you imagine might happen. It's a personal response: after all, if two people are in the exact same situation only one may experience fear. Fear can also be associated with the prehistoric part of your brain, such that when it takes over, your fight or flight response is triggered.

Most things you fear in everyday life are not really life threatening at all, but this makes little difference to the prehistoric part of your brain. Whether the fear is triggered when you are asked to stand up and do a presentation, or when speaking to someone you don't know, or doing something genuinely dangerous, it's all the same to your prehistoric mind.

Fear responses are learned over time, by seeing things our parents react to, experiencing scary situations or hearing about them from other people. So to reduce or remove the fear, you need to go about changing the thoughts and feelings associated with the formula:

Thoughts → Feelings → Action → Results

You need to reduce or remove the emotional tug that fear has on you because that's what holds you back.

How much fear do you have?

When it comes to starting a difficult conversation, or a conversation with people you don't know, how much fear do you feel? It's important to understand how much fear you feel in a given situation. For many people, the fear doesn't have to be totally eliminated in order for them to take action – it just needs to come down to a comfortable level.

For some people, fear is part of the process and they will push on even with a moderate to high level of it. For others, even just a small amount is enough to hold them back. If, in the past, you have achieved something despite an element of fear, you are likely to have a higher fear tolerance. As you've carried on despite fear in the past, your mindset could be that fear isn't a reason to hold back and not take action.

Let go of your fear

A really good exercise you can do right now is to score the level of fear you currently experience in different situations. Once you've established a baseline, you can measure your progress when you next take action regardless of the fear or undertake exercises to reduce that fear.

We'll be measuring fear using something called a SUD level, which stands for Subjective Unit of Distress (or as I like to call it – Discomfort). The SUD-level was developed by Joseph Wolpe in 1969.

You measure this yourself; it is your own scale and totally unique to you.

You don't necessarily need to be in the actual fear situation to work out your SUD level in a given scenario. Just sitting down, relaxing and imagining the situation should be enough to give you a good sense of how much fear you would experience.

The way it works is as follows.

When you are in a situation and you experience fear ask yourself:

"How scared am I? How high is my level of fear on a scale of 0–10 where 0 is 'It's not a problem at all,

---

I could do it in my sleep' and 10 is 'I know for certain I will die if I do this'."

These steps will help you measure your fear levels:

1. Remember the last time you were in the situation that you fear.
2. Visualize in your mind what you saw at that time.
3. Imagine you can hear any sounds you heard or things you remember people saying or you said to yourself.
4. Ask yourself – "How much fear did I have in that situation on a scale of 0–10?"

If you are struggling to experience the fear in your imagination, then you just need to put yourself into the situation that causes the fear and take the measurement. For example, if for you it's talking to people you don't know, then try the following exercise:

1. Go somewhere where there are lots of people around.
2. Tell yourself you are going to force yourself to speak to someone.
3. Think of something to say or a question to ask – even **"Have you got the time please?"**
4. Start to walk in their direction.
5. Speak to them.

Whether you do actually speak to them or not, it doesn't matter. The important thing is to take your SUD reading by asking yourself: "What was that fear level on a scale of 0–10?"

It doesn't matter what your number currently is. It's a reference point for you and you alone. Now, when you start to work through the book, you can take your SUD level at regular intervals and notice your progress.

For some people, knowing that they've got the skillset to start and maintain a conversation and deal with difficult situations is enough for them to begin starting conversations despite their fear levels or SUD reading. For others though, the uncomfortable fear feeling that comes up still needs to be addressed and brought down to a more manageable level on their SUD scale. That's what we are going to be looking at next.

Fear and anxiety

It's important to understand the difference between fear and anxiety.

Fear is generally based on a definite situation that is actually happening right now. For instance, someone says to you "Stand up and tell us all about what you have been up to this last week". If this is something you'd hate to do, then you'd experience fear in that situation.

Anxiety, on the other hand, is a little different – although it manifests itself with very similar symptoms and feelings to fear. Anxiety is worrying about a situation in the future that may not ever happen. It can be helpful to shift the dialogue from saying you have a fear of something, to saying you are anxious about it instead. For many people this transition can make the situation they're about to go through less daunting.

Ways to reduce your fear or push on regardless

There are a number of different ways to reduce your SUD score. Different techniques work better for different people.

1. You might find that gaining a skillset in a particular area you fear helps you push through your fear. When you repeat the activity, the fear diminishes further and further and in most cases goes away completely. It may not get to 0, but a 1 or 2 on a SUD scale is low enough for most people to get on with life. A small amount of fear is natural and normal to most people and perfectly healthy.
2. Fear is based on how you think about things and, in most situations, how you imagine things playing out. One simple way of reducing fear is to imagine the situation differently. Try imagining the situation you fear in a similar way to something you don't fear. For instance, I knew my fear of public speaking was made worse because I imagined everything going wrong. By comparison, I didn't fear sales meetings, I liked them. However, with

sales meetings I realized I always thought about things going well. I then used the same technique with speaking, i.e. I stopped thinking about all that could go wrong, and instead developed the habit of thinking about things going well. I also noticed my inner voice was upbeat when thinking about sales meetings, but down and dreary when thinking about speaking. I changed that as well: just by catching myself talking in my head in the dreary voice, then repeating the same words again but with the upbeat internal voice. When you change the thought pattern, you change the feelings and the feelings are where the fear exists. It can be useful to consult a hypnotherapist or NLP specialist to help you change your thought patterns in this way.

NLP works by helping you change your think-ing patterns so that you think about things in a way that generates a more positive emotion, or at least a reduced negative emotion. As with hypnotherapy, NLP is something that is best done with a qualified NLP practitioner, although there are many techniques that you can develop and use yourself.

3. Another way to reduce fear, anxiety and other negative emotions is through a "body awareness" exercise that you can do very easily with a little practice. The actual process itself is very, very simple and explained in the next exercise. This is all about dealing with emotions directly – dealing at a feelings level with that fear and releasing it.

Exercise: Body Awareness for Dealing with Your Fear

It isn't the thoughts you have that hold you back, it is the resulting fear emotion that you feel in your stomach or somewhere in your body when you have those thoughts that causes you to stop. What if you could just stop that feeling of fear or emotional response from happening? You can do this by following some really ancient lessons.

Our minds are constantly "on". Even in the middle of a task, part of your mind will be imagining future scenarios or replaying past events. In fact, your mind, like most people's, probably spends most of the time thinking about the future and the past and very little time focused in the exact moment you are currently living.

So why is this important? Well, most of the anxiety that you experience is based on thinking about future things that haven't happened yet or may not happen. Meditation encourages you to be present in the current moment but the reality is that not many people can do that. Try this technique for interrupting your mind's stream of consciousness:

→ When you notice your mind is running away on autopilot in a stream of negative thoughts, engage your conscious mind and ask yourself:

"Why am I thinking this?"
"Why am I doing this to myself? Is it helping me? I don't have to do this right now!"

→ Become aware of any fear feeling or anxiety about the runaway thoughts.

OR:

When a fear comes up or anxiety starts, ask yourself:

"What must I be thinking in order to feel like this?"
"What was I just thinking about before I started to feel nervous or uncomfortable?"

Once you have got used to interrupting your mind's flow, you are ready to move to the next stage.

Follow these steps when you notice you are thinking about things incessantly or worrying about something:

1. Notice the thoughts you are having.
2. Stop yourself by bringing your attention back into the current moment – where you are and what you are doing.
3. Notice how your feet feel on the floor.
4. Notice what your arms feel like, your breathing and the noises that you can hear in the environment.
5. Focus as much as you can on the present moment that you are in and simply notice the negative thoughts that you are having and observe them without getting dragged into them, perhaps just saying something to yourself like: **"Oh, I don't need to think about that right now"**. Or, my favourite one when I notice my thoughts running

away with themselves is to simply say to myself **"There it is"** – not with any judgement or criticism – just an observational statement: **"There it is"**. In that split second when you realize what your mind is doing, you are in the current moment.

Remember: start to notice when your mind is running away with itself and observe it. Get used to the idea that this is what your mind does and understand that you don't have to be dragged into it. You can say, **"Hey. There it is"** or **"I don't need to think about this right now"** and move your attention somewhere else. A great idea is to get up and go and do something to take your attention away.

Fear feelings send us into a panic cycle which perpetuates the fear. We end up thinking more and more about the situation causing the fear, building it up more and more dramatically in our minds. The fear feeling becomes blocked and stuck in our system. To reduce and remove this fear feeling, follow this simple process, refining the technique you practised in the previous exercise.

The more you do this exercise, the better you will become at it. You are allowing the emotion to flow without resistance and without adding to it. At the same time you are preventing your mind from focusing on the thoughts causing that feeling, making yourself feel worse and worse.

1. Notice when you get any sort of uncomfortable, uneasy fear feeling come up – even the small ones that might arise in normal day-to-day life.
2. Notice them and, when they occur, just focus on the feeling fully.
3. Feel it; focus on it *without* letting your mind run away with whatever you were thinking about that caused that fear feeling. Instead, concentrate on the fear feeling; just observe it as a sensation in your body and allow it to be there.
4. Don't resist it, think of it like you would an itch – you notice it as a body sensation but it doesn't trigger a negative thought cycle of doom and gloom – it's just a sensation.
5. Allow it to be there and simply say to yourself – **"Oh, there it is: that feeling"** – and as you focus on it, it will very often gradually fade away.

At the moment, you probably have a natural reaction to the fear feeling; you end up thinking about the thing you're fearful of even more and perpetuating it. By doing these exercises, you will break the self-perpetuating cycle. Like most things in life it does takes practice and time to get the best results. At first you may not think it's making any difference at all – but stay with it.

These exercises are the basis of most of the spiritual and healthy living teachings through the ages, which tell you to notice your thoughts or feelings but not to get dragged into them. By doing this, you start to become more present – because you can only ever take action in the current moment. You can't do anything yesterday and you can't do anything tomorrow (yet). You need to take your mind off the past and the future and focus on the moment in hand, as that is the point where you can make a difference and change things.

Your Mindset – The Biggest Potential Barrier

The biggest potential barrier to successful communication is you and your mindset. The meaning you attach to the responses you get will have a huge bearing on how you build your communication skills. You may have heard it said that it's not what happens to you in life – it's the meaning that you attach to it.

If you tried to talk to someone and they looked away, what meaning would you attach to that?

You may think you've done something wrong, and conclude that starting conversations with people you don't know is unacceptable. If you internalize that meaning you are unlikely to have much of an appetite for starting conversations with people in the future. But what if they were just shy? Maybe they were upset or having a bad day. If you attach this meaning to it, you'd have a very different outcome.

This shift in your mindset is what can help to overcome the fear around talking to absolutely anyone.

Conclusion

Fear is not real. It is an emotional reaction *that you do to yourself* under certain circumstances. This could be either when something is actually happening or when you think about something that might happen in the future. Your emotional pattern or reaction is based on out-of-date experiences from a time when you didn't have all the resources you have today. In most cases, fears were developed when you were a child in situations that caused you distress. As a child you did not have the ability, the voice or the logical reasoning to stand up for yourself or deal fully with situations.

Scientists believe we are only born with two fears: the fear of loud noises and the fear of falling. That means that all the other fears you've developed over time are learned – through observing what happens to other people, watching television, reading books and, of course, your own life experiences.

It is your thoughts that cause your anxieties and fears, so a great starting point to overcoming those fears is to develop a better awareness of your own thoughts and emotions.

Remember not to let fear stop you making progress or taking action. Yes, you may need to reduce the fear level on your SUD scale to get to a point where you feel you can push on and take action, but you now have the tools to work on this.

Many people take action regardless of fear, even if it is quite a high SUD, because they know they really want the outcome. I once heard someone say that courage is mastery of fear and not the absence of fear – something worth remembering.

Finally, notice when thoughts drag you to the past or project you into the future and become aware of that – just notice it. You will probably be surprised how often it happens when you start observing. Focusing on the present moment will help retrain your mind to do this past and future projection less frequently. We associate different feelings with different words, and just quietly and calmly saying the word "**relax**" to yourself a few times can really help your body start that process. Fear doesn't exist when you are relaxed.

2
"I Don't Want to Experience Rejection"

One of the biggest reasons why people don't speak up, or ask for something, or talk to somebody they don't know, is fear of rejection. This stems from not knowing how to handle what appeared to be rejection, if it happened, and goes back to childhood for most people. As a child, when you get into trouble, you can't defend your position because it's an adult, teacher or parent, telling you off. You just have to take it: feeling humiliated and embarrassed. As an adult though, you can stand your own ground in a calm, confident and friendly manner. You no longer have to fear vulnerability from rejection.

When approaching someone to start a conversation, fear of rejection returns in the form of the fear of getting a bad response. But how rational is that fear? If the person you're talking to is shy, they might ignore you or look away, but that's down to their own shyness not you. If they're confident, they'll probably engage with you or at least answer you.

It's highly unlikely that you're going to get a bad response in either situation.

I remember working with one client who had a fear of speaking to new people. He had this fear because he believed other people would see his attempts to start a conversation as proof that he was sad and lonely and didn't have any friends. I pointed out that no one could possibly come to this conclusion with the little information they had. He could have had a coach load of friends outside for all they knew. When someone starts talking it is more likely that they will simply be seen as a chatty, friendly, confident person. Once my client realized this, his thoughts changed and his actions changed too.

"Sorry. Am I in your way?"

Have you ever had somebody push past you in a crowded environment? How did it make you feel? Maybe you felt like the other person had abused your presence or attempted to bully or dominate you. Next time it happens, turn around and say, **"Sorry. Am I in your way?"** in a friendly, curious inquisitive tone. Even if they ignore you, you will feel like you dealt with the situation.

Very often saying nothing causes you to feel like you've been trodden on. So instead of thinking, "Well they're rude", or "They just felt like they could bully or push me around", respond to the situation in this way instead and you'll feel as if you stood your ground. The key with this though is to be genuinely curious, and not sarcastic, otherwise it might be taken as a passive aggressive response. Some people might believe this is still passive aggressive, we all believe different things. This approach has always worked well for me personally and always had a positive outcome. The meaning is in the tonality used, not the words said.

We all live by different beliefs, values and experiences. And most of the time when people think they've been rejected, they haven't been at all.

When you start a conversation with someone, you never know exactly how they feel at that point in time and what mood they are in, apart from very obvious signs of course.

Their mood or state of mind is one of the most important factors in how they respond to you. The response that you get to anything in life is based on:

→ Where the other person is at that point in time.
→ What has happened to them recently or that day.
→ What is going on in their life.
→ The impact or consequence it has to them, whether real or perceived.
→ What you said or did in relation to what else is going on in their life at the time.

The best way to overcome a fear of rejection is to add two new skills to your skillset: how to approach and what to say (both covered in Part Two). You also need to develop your mindset around rejection and realize that, even if it happens, it is not *you* being rejected. Instead, it is your actions, your views or your ideas. If an idea, action or view is rejected, it doesn't mean you are wrong; it just means the other person has a different point of view, which may be based on the mindset and place that person is in at that point in time.

Of course you can, to some degree, judge who looks like they might welcome a conversation. For instance, say there are two people standing separately and you, for whatever reason, need to ask a question. If one of them is looking around half smiling and the other one has their arms crossed with a frown on their face, which one do you think it is best to approach and talk to?

The easiest and "lowest risk" style of interaction is the "in motion" interaction. As you are walking along, make a general, throwaway, passing comment. In this situation even if there is no response from the other person, it doesn't matter. You do not risk standing there with no reciprocation from the other person, wishing you'd never actually opened your mouth. In reality, providing you make a non-threatening, friendly approach and you've correctly read the signs that someone is approachable, the chances of getting no feedback at all or of somebody being rude to you are very, very remote.

Adopt a positive mindset.

> To avoid thinking "I'll either get a good outcome or a bad outcome", instead say to yourself:
>
> **"This is either going to go brilliantly or there'll be an amazing story to tell people later about how I spoke to someone and got a really weird response."**

When, on reflection, you can see the funny side of a conversation that hasn't gone particularly well, you'll realize that it's no big deal if it doesn't go to plan. If you get ignored, go and tell five people you know. Say, **"Hey you'll never guess what happened to me today. I wish the ground had opened up."** When it becomes an amusing story, you don't even take it seriously yourself any more. This is a great stage to get to because it gives you a new way of thinking about starting conversations and removes much of the hesitation that can hold you back.

A "good enough reason" to overcome hesitation

A common reason for holding back from speaking to new people is the feeling that there isn't a good enough reason to speak to them. So why, then, does anyone speak to someone they don't know? What could their "good enough" reasons be?

→ Perhaps they're showing the world they're a great, friendly, confident person.

→ Maybe they want to lighten an awkward situation or stop others feeling uncomfortable.

→ They might want to be helpful; aid someone they see struggling.

→ They may want to just pass the time when there's nothing else to do or find out more about something they're interested in.

→ They could be practising the art you're learning in this book.

23

My hope is that as you read this book and grow in confidence, you'll look for opportunities to put into practice what you've learned and continually prove to yourself how far you've come. You'll be doing something that will enrich your life immensely. When you stop worrying about rejection, because it doesn't exist anyway, you can get out there and interact with people and enjoy lots of new opportunities as a result.

It's a good idea to develop some new beliefs and tell yourself that starting conversations with people is fun. Opening a conversation is all an adventure: it is a game to see what happens and how you can develop it.

Years ago I had a belief that stopped me talking to people I didn't know. I thought that if I spoke to people, it would make me look sad or vulnerable and that would give them control over me or the situation.

I broke that cycle by developing a new belief: by speaking to people, I *would* be in control. I realized there was no way I could be thought of as vulnerable when I can speak to anyone, anywhere and always make a new friend.

Fear of rejection is a reason some people have for not speaking to others. As you've discovered, it's a fear that has no grounding in reality. You may not get the response you expect and you may, in rare circumstances, be ignored, but you've learned new strategies for coping with these scenarios here. Now is the time to try them out.

3
"I Worry about What Other People Might Think"

Have you ever walked into a room and felt like every single person is looking at you? Some people take this to the extreme and become highly sensitive and embarrassed about walking into any public situation, imagining that the whole room is looking at them and judging them. No doubt you've already heard this said before . . .

People have got far too much going on in their own lives to be worried about what you're doing or what you're getting up to. Nobody is thinking about you as much as you think they are!

Even so, when you walk into a room, some people are bound to look up. Does that mean everyone is looking at you and disapproving of you? Actually, what *is* going on here is something quite different.

It's human nature to look up or glance over, regardless of who's just come into the room. It's one of our inbuilt defence mechanisms to protect us from danger when something comes into our environment. "Friend or foe?" It's a subconscious reaction to ensure the coast is clear.

There could be other explanations too. Maybe people are looking round as you enter simply because they are waiting to meet someone. Of all the reasons people might glance up, 99.9% of the time it will have nothing whatsoever to do with you!

What Others Might Think of Your Interaction

A lot of people get concerned about talking to somebody they don't know in public. They worry about what people around them will think when they see them talking to a "stranger". What you need to remember is that people nearby do not know whether you know that person or not. The only people that know there is no existing relationship for sure are you and the person you are talking to. So worrying about what bystanders may think needn't be an issue.

Often, someone who worries what other people think will also worry about making a mistake, looking stupid or getting something wrong. This goes back to the classic fear of failure where you assume you're no good at something just because the immediate outcome isn't fantastic. But there's a learning curve to everything in life. You can't expect to do things perfectly first time. Focus instead on how your results improve with practice.

Your time for living is now, not some time in the future. So, start doing more of the things you want to do today and worry less (or not at all) about what others may think. The likelihood is that they're not thinking about you anyway.

Lots of people have low self-esteem and lack confidence to some degree or another. Often you wouldn't realize it to look at them. The common trait in pretty much all of the thousands of people I've worked with and mentored one to one is that they lack confidence. And that includes hugely successful people who hold senior positions in very large corporations. You see, we're all sensitive to one degree or another, but we show it in different ways. Often we overcompensate by looking more confident than we really are. In most situations the person you're talking to is likely to be looking for *your* approval as well, so they're unlikely to be judging you harshly.

Let's play devil's advocate though. Let's say someone is judging or criticizing you. Ask yourself these questions:

→ Who are they to do so?
→ What have they done or achieved to allow them to do that?
→ Are they qualified to judge you?

No. Nothing makes them good enough to judge you.

You're your own person. You make your own decisions and take your own actions. Just because someone doesn't agree with you or approve of what you may be doing doesn't make it wrong. It's right for you.

Important

When I say to stop worrying about what other people think and do what you want, this is within a specific within limits. The limit is that you can do what you want as long as it does not harm another person's enjoyment of their own life or experiences. What? I hear you say. I mean you can't be someone that is loud and rude in a public place, like a quiet restaurant, and feel it is OK because you now don't care what others think. We apply the idea of not worrying or caring what others think to aspects of our life that are constrained, and where we are held back from normal things that we can see others doing in general everyday life, but without upsetting others.

Handling the fear of criticism

A good approach is to imagine the worst happening and then imagine yourself dealing with it. By doing this, you can tick a box in your mind against the fear, which will help you eliminate it or at least scale it down. For instance, you might imagine people laughing at you when you get something wrong, and then imagine yourself saying to the people that are laughing **"I'm really glad you liked that"** in an amusing, sarcastic way; or **"I'm glad I put a smile on your face"**. Or if somebody gets angry and has a go at you in front of others, you could imagine yourself turning round and saying **"Okay, that's interesting"**. Think of yourself as a stand-up comedian dealing with hecklers.

These responses show that you haven't taken their reaction to heart – you haven't let the situation or their response intimidate you.

Conclusion

Make sure you pay attention to your inner voice and the things you are saying to yourself. Ask yourself **"Are these things constructive and moving me in the direction I want to go, or is there another way of looking at this?"**

I overcame an intense fear of public speaking. I used to worry about what others would think if I got up and spoke in public. I feared rejection and worried about making mistakes. I have now reached the stage where I love speaking in public. I can speak to a thousand people with no notes or slides and I love every minute of it. How did I get to this point? By doing exactly what I'm telling you. I'd imagine it going well. I'd imagine people liking what I was doing. I practised on my own at home or in my office. I practised how I would say things. I pretended it didn't bother me when I got up to speak and I told myself that people would like me. I kept telling myself that I was good at it. I got really proud that I could do something so easily that others found really hard. I felt proud that I could do it and that was a great motivator for me to go ahead and make the most of a situation where I had previously worried what other people might think.

When you worry too much about what other people think, you are in real danger of missing out on what you could achieve. You, too, can change your beliefs about yourself and be amazed at how you can transform your life and results in a short period of time.

4
"I Hate Talking to Strangers – Why Would I Want to?"

Most of us grow up with an inbuilt negativity towards speaking to strangers. During your formative years, your parents may have warned you to stay away from strangers, for instance. Maybe those messages still affect how you feel and act in certain situations today.

I remember a number of years ago talking with a friend about this exact thing. He told me that to go and sit in a coffee shop on his own, surrounded by people he didn't know, was one of the worst situations he could imagine. Going to a pub or bar where he didn't know anyone, on the other hand, was not an issue at all. His beliefs told him that a coffee shop is somewhere people go to meet with friends, whereas a bar is where conversation with new people (i.e. strangers) is acceptable.

This was the exact opposite of what my own belief system used to be back then. I could quite happily have a coffee alone, but for me, anyone that went into a pub on their own obviously didn't have any friends! Of course I no longer have that belief.

Can you see how your beliefs affect the way you see things and the way you live your life?

> **So what is it for you? What aspects of life or situations do you find uncomfortable or difficult in the presence of strangers?**
>
> It might be worth thinking about this for a few minutes and making a list. This list will highlight the areas you need to work on as you go through the rest of this book.

This chapter looks at how you could think about strangers in a different way. It will enable you to develop and build your "speaking to strangers muscles". A good analogy is that of a workout: the ability to strike up conversations, and be comfortable and relaxed about it, takes consistent practice over a period of time.

Why Bother Talking to Strangers Anyway?

First, let's deal with the "why bother?" question. The term "strangers" itself is a funny one. We are all human beings, having the same experience of living. We all breathe, talk and eat. It might be helpful to think of "strangers" just as people you don't yet know; potential friends. Think about it. Other than your immediate family, anyone else that has given you a job, given you a pay rise, made you smile, made you laugh or you've fallen in love with was once a stranger!

There must be more people like them out there!

Once you're able to speak to people you do not know, and initiate conversations with them, your whole life will expand, you will be more comfortable and relaxed in social and business situations, you will have better experiences and you will learn far more about the world and other people.

A mundane daily chore can become an adventure when you meet and engage with someone new who is interesting, even if that adventure only lasts a minute or two.

It might sound like a cliché but the world *will* become your oyster, and you *will* start to enjoy everyday situations, just because you can!

You Already Speak to More Strangers Than You Think

Like most people, you probably do speak to strangers when either the connection or reason to do so is good enough. Let's look at some examples of this.

→ You are running late for a very important appointment and you are not sure which way to go. You may not normally ask a stranger for directions, but on this occasion, because your need is big enough, you override your usual hesitation.

→ Your car won't start. You are stranded and in need of help from anyone who's around.

→ You are away in a strange country where the language spoken is not your native tongue. You are waiting for a train and you hear a voice from your own country. You ask them where they are from and start a conversation like you were long lost friends.

→ You are away on holiday and staying in a small family-run hotel. As you go down to breakfast, you smile at the other guests. Perhaps you say **"Good morning"** and even engage them in some general conversation about the weather or the hotel.

→ You are standing in a crowded place where you do not know anyone else. All of a sudden a car backfires, and you and the people near you look at each other and start talking about what has just happened.

Most of us will engage in conversation with a stranger when the reason or need is great enough and we can see no other alternative. It is also the case that we will engage in conversation with a stranger when we feel there is enough of a connection or commonality between us.

So, in the examples of staying in a hotel, being in a strange country or something dramatic happening in the environment, most people feel a connection to others through their shared experience.

If you have an internal rule that says you can only speak to someone else when there is a good enough connection, one quick way to become more open to striking up conversations is to adjust your criteria of what is a good enough connection. You might extend it to include being in the same place at the same time, and engaging in a similar activity. Suddenly, you've opened up a whole new set of connections, such as everyday occurrences like waiting for a bus or train, walking across the car park to the ticket machine, browsing around the same shop and attending the same event.

Ask yourself what really is the difference between these everyday occurrences and the list given earlier.

Make a shortlist now of public situations you are regularly in where you could start to talk to people you don't know, even if it is just a pleasant comment or statement.

Start easy. Shop assistants are great for practice. It's a safe environment and – guess what? – they're paid to speak to customers! That is their job.

Knowing isn't Doing

I want you to read this section as many times as you have to, until you understand it. Knowing isn't the same as doing. In the earlier section I asked you to do an exercise and make a list. Did you do it or just think about it?

If you just thought about it, this is nothing like making the list physically. The same with any exercises I ask you to do. If you read them and think – "I've got that, great", then you are unlikely to make progress.

You have to do the exercises and think about what you have written or done – that's the magic to change. Too many people don't actually do the exercises and wonder why change hasn't happened for them.

Conclusion

There is a limit to how much you can grow as a person or grow your success and happiness in life with the people you currently know. The simple fact is – most of your future success and personal growth depends on people you do not yet know. If you can work on changing your mindset and how you feel about talking to strangers, you will open up a whole world of new opportunities for yourself.

Anybody you start speaking to could end up being an employer, a customer or a lifetime friend. You need to be open to communication, whether in "random situations", like a bookshop, a coffee shop, the supermarket or a sporting event, or in business situations, such as a conference, training course or seminar. There are so many opportunities out there once you start expanding your horizons and your contact base to include the people that you don't (yet) know. If you are still hesitant about speaking to new people, there may be other reasons at play here. A lot of the time you might not know what to say or how to say it. That's covered in Part Two of the book, where you will work through the four main stages of an interaction.

PART TWO

The Four Stages of an Interaction

5
Stage 1 – Your Outcome and Starting a Conversation

Without initiating a conversation, nothing else can happen. This is the most important, and usually the most difficult, step.

Once you know how to start a conversation with someone you don't know, you'll be able to develop the rest of your skills and start achieving fantastic results.

As well as learning how to start a conversation, in this stage we will also look at:

→ Understanding the outcome you want.
→ How to handle different business and social environments.
→ Who looks open to conversation and who does not?

Most of the focus in this first stage is on starting a conversation with a stranger. There will be times when it's difficult to talk to people you already know, of course, and, in those situations, the same strategies apply.

When you start practising your new skills, do whatever is most comfortable for you. You might prefer to be on your own, but if you need the backup of friends, that's fine. Do whatever feels best to you, but whatever you do, keep practising.

Know the Outcome You Want!

So what outcome do you want from this communication? Is this business or social? Is this casual or is there something else you would like to happen?

Some example outcomes might be:

- → Ease an awkward situation.
- → Find out some information you need.
- → Connect and share experiences with someone who looks to be into the same things as you.
- → Share an interesting moment.
- → Get a sale.
- → Meet someone who could help you.
- → Get friends to agree to a trip.
- → Stop a team member at work making mistakes.
- → How about just being nice and brightening someone's day!

Knowing your desired outcome before starting a conversation is essential. Let's say you have a team member at work who isn't doing their job properly and keeps making mistakes. You need to speak to them, but what do you want to happen as a result?

Do you want them to be so upset and frustrated that they start looking for a new job?

Or

Do you want them to mend their ways and do things properly in the future?

The words and tone you use will determine which of those two routes they go down.

1. If you were looking for the first outcome, you would probably just criticize all they had done and let them know they were not up to the job. (Not my advised route, especially with a new team member or someone on a learning curve!)
2. If you wanted them to get things done properly in future, then you would more likely ask them how "we could make sure things go better in future" and what you could do to help them.

By deciding the outcome before you start the conversation you can choose the appropriate words, tone and approach.

For another example, think of how you might decide the outcome you want from a business networking event. It would not be advisable, for instance, for your desired outcome to be just "to find people to sell to". It might not be particularly effective to have this expectation influencing your approach and words. A more beneficial outcome could be "to connect with some like-minded people of quality to build synergies for the future". Part of your desired outcome might be to get a date in the diary to meet up, so that you can discuss more about what you both do and how you could potentially help each other in the future.

Knowing your outcome helps you plan ahead and direct the conversation. It also means you can set realistic expectations and relax more, because you know your goal.

Being Clear about Your Reasons for the Interaction

When you start an interaction with somebody a few things go through their mind, the first of which is likely to be "What does this person want and why are they talking to me?" Of course, this may be more obvious to them in some situations, such as at a sporting event, where you are both having the same experience and casual conversation is often made. However, this can differ in a more general public situation, such as a book or coffee shop scenario. Often, when you start talking to somebody that you don't know, they may – on a conscious or subconscious level – be wondering "What is this all about? Why are you talking to me and what do you want?"

If you've anticipated these concerns, you can eliminate them in your opening statement or question and put the other person at ease. For instance, let's say you are in a bookshop and you need some advice about finding a suitable cookery book for a gift. You see another shopper looking through the cookery section too. You could just ask them, **"What's a good cookery book?"** – and you'd probably get an answer. But the blunt approach doesn't fully address the "Why are you asking me and what do you want?" question.

If instead you said, **"Excuse me, you look like somebody who is into cookery. Could you recommend a good book for a beginner? It's my cousin's birthday next week and I want to get him a book because he's expressed an interest in cookery."** You have now acknowledged why you are asking them (they look like they're into cookery because they're in the cookery section too) and what you're after (advice because your cousin is interested in cookery). So, in this example, you have immediately crossed off a number of conscious or subconscious concerns the other person might have about you speaking to them in that moment.

Another thought that may go through the other person's mind is "How long will this take, am I going to be stuck with this person?" Ask yourself, will you need to chat for a long time to get your desired outcome or is this a short interaction? Again, this could be determined in an opening statement, something like, **"Excuse me, I've got a quick question for you."** This reassures the other person that this will just be a fleeting encounter – there is no need for them to be alarmed or concerned, or start worrying about how long it might take.

In some situations the reason you are starting a conversation or asking a question is obvious. For instance, if you were walking through a car park and you saw somebody getting into a particular car that you liked, you might say to them, **"Hi there. I am thinking of getting one of those pretty soon. I just wondered, how do you find it? Is it practical to drive every day?"** In this situation you don't have to acknowledge that they own the car you want because it's obvious from the question. What you want from them is obvious too because you are asking their opinion on their own car. In this instance, the number of potential concerns or reasons you need to address up front is reduced because most things are obvious and implied by the situation.

So, remember it's not just about what you say; it is about considering how else it could be interpreted. What you don't say – secondary communication – is also important, as mentioned in the Introduction.

What you could do in any situation is establish in your mind:

> "How many reasons are they going to have in their head?"
> "What are they going to be wondering about?"
> and
> "How can I put them at ease with my opening statement?"

How you start a conversation also depends on the environment you are in, which we will now explore. We will look at various types of environment in turn, with examples of how to get started with your conversation in each one.

When/Where – Based on the Environment

One of the key factors affecting the dynamics of an interaction is the environment. This has a bearing on how you might start a conversation, as well as what you might say.

So, first off, let's start with what most people find the most difficult situation of all; speaking to a totally random stranger in a very public or general environment.

The random stranger in a very public environment

Public situations would include the supermarket, a coffee shop or bookshop, waiting at the bus stop, or taking a lift or elevator. In these situations we usually have no pre-set agenda or real outcome, nor do we have any known common ground with the person we are about to talk to.

First, though, let's review why you might want to talk to anyone in these situations in the first place. As you've read before, this book's premise is that meeting new people, on a regular basis, creates new opportunities for your social life, your business life and your success. Unless you are open to interactions, you will never create new opportunities for yourself. Plus, it's just dead time otherwise! Why just stand in line waiting for a coffee when you could fill the time with something more interesting?

So take the opportunity whenever you can to talk to new people. Strike up a conversation with somebody nearby who looks like they might be open to a conversation and see where it takes you. Your desired outcome could simply be to do something with the moment, to brighten someone's day or pass the time and have an experience that would otherwise have been missed. It could be as simple as that.

Breaking the deadly silence in a lift or elevator

A classic situation is the lift or elevator. It's a fact that most (or all) of us find being in an elevator with a group of people we don't know very awkward. People will do anything to avoid eye contact, usually simply staring at the panel as the floor indicators light up.

What do you think happens if somebody says something to lighten the atmosphere? It all changes, partly because everyone's just breathing a sigh of relief that they're not standing in a lift with an axe murderer! I always say something in this situation, and the outcome I'm looking for, the reason I do it, is easing an otherwise difficult situation.

The most common thing I do is look for the sign that says the maximum number of people that can fit into that lift. As we all know those numbers are very ambitious – we can be crowded in a lift with six people and look up to see that the capacity of that lift is actually twenty people!

So, I'll look for that and, while looking up at the sign, say:

"I don't know how you get twenty people in here; that must be fun!"

Sometimes people engage and say a response; other times they just smile or acknowledge my comment. Regardless of their level of response, the situation has been lightened and I feel good, in fact I feel proud that I was "brave enough" to speak in an environment where people generally don't!

Other Environments

There are many other environments that we find ourselves in outside of the general, random public encounter that we've just explored. Here are some more that we commonly find ourselves in, although of course there are many others.

The recreational event

When you're at a sports event, the theatre, the cinema – anywhere like this – you obviously have the common ground that you are both at the event in the same way that other people are. Good questions to ask people to start a conversation are things like:

"What other events like this have you been to?"
"What did you think of the event last week?"
"What did you think of the cup final last week?"
(If it's a sporting event and there was a cup final last week!)

What you should notice here is that I said, **"What did you think of the cup final last week?"** and not "Did you *see* the cup final last week?" The latter is at risk of leading to just a yes or no response, which is something you should avoid where possible. By saying, **"What did you think . . . ?"** you are more likely to have started a conversation. Even if they just say, "I didn't see it" you can then come back with, **"Oh, you had better things on, did you? What did you get up to then?"** Avoiding yes or no responses is key to engaging people in conversation.

Remember to ask interesting questions:

→ What their experience was like.
→ How they did something.
→ How they felt in a situation.

These are all ways to generate interesting responses and interesting responses lead to easier conversations for both parties.

The learning event

A learning event could be a course or a seminar – something like that. In these situations you can ask people if they have done much on this topic before, what other similar courses or seminars they've been to and what they thought of them, whether this course was recommended by somebody or if they have attended this course before. There are many different ways you can open a conversation, with a connection having been established through being at the same learning event.

The business event

A great opener for a networking event is simply to go up to somebody, introduce yourself and ask them **"What keeps you busy during the week then?"** I love this opening compared to the classic "What do you do?" which seems a bit more direct. Opening up with **"What keeps you busy during the week then?"** also gives the other person the opportunity not just to talk about their work or career but to expand into what they do outside of work.

Business meetings generally follow a particular format. Before a meeting begins there is often a little rapport building or general day-to-day chitchat. Very often people will ask you what your journey was like and things like that. I find a great way of starting a conversation at a meeting is to comment on the parking – if they have good parking facilities that is. I'll simply say something like, **"You know what? I am going to come here again. It's so easy to park – one of the best places I've been to"** – and this will typically engage them in a conversation about how hard it is to park at certain places, and so on.

In a meeting situation, the chitchat will generally go on for a short period of time until the magical moment occurs where you all go into business mode. Up until that point is the general rapport-building conversation. Good conversational topics in this situation can be things like, **"Have you got anything exciting planned for this weekend?"** or **"Did you get up to anything exciting at the weekend?"**

Always be observant, looking at what photographs they may have on their desk or on their walls, for clues about what interests them and use this to open up a conversation about one of their passions. As soon as you can, draw people into conversations about their passions, that is when they really do lock-in on the engagement front. Not only that, by talking about something they enjoy or like, you put them in a good frame of mind and emotional state.

The social event

Social events, like parties or dinner parties, are different occasions altogether. In this situation, one of the easiest ways to get speaking to people that you have not met before is simply to ask them **"So how do you know the host?"** I think it's a fair assumption that if you are at a party you probably know or have been introduced to the host by somebody. The other person may well tell you a short story about when they met the host or how they know each other. Perhaps they grew up as children together or work together – any of these are great areas in which to expand a conversation and get engagement.

A holiday or trip

While you're on holiday you can generally start a conversation using small talk. Simply asking people where they live and what it's like there, or whether they've been to this particular place before, are good ways to get people talking about their holiday, their trip or their experiences back home.

Who – Who Do We Talk to Based on Who Looks Approachable?

In addition to having an outcome in mind before initiating a conversation, it is also a good idea to develop the skill of making a judgement call on who looks open to a conversation or, just as important, who doesn't look like they'd welcome one.

Although it is really just common sense, most people don't think of this. In the emotional turmoil of starting a conversation all logic goes out the window. Very often when people try and connect and it doesn't work, they blame themselves.

This section highlights some of the reasons communication may not go well.

Signs that "now may be a good time" to start a conversation

It is likely that people who are open to communication are more confident and friendly, have a strong presence and are noisier in any situation; they are more expressive, you know they are there. So, for example, they may stand behind you and see the long line in the bank and say to themselves out loud **"Oh, no, another long wait"**, or exclaim about the cold weather. These can, in most cases, be taken as invitations to connect by responding to them. You can also start to do these extra animations, sighs or comments to yourself in situations where you want others to talk to you, to start creating your own under-the-radar "invitations to connect". We explore all the ways of starting a conversation in Chapters 6 and 7, as well as how to handle the different responses you might get.

The best time to engage with people is when they are in a "stuck state", i.e. they are not going anywhere in that minute or two because of circumstances around them. While you're waiting at a pedestrian crossing or a train platform, or standing in line at a store for example – you are both literally stuck until the situation moves forward. These are good situations in which to engage with someone new and practise your conversation skills, because they have literally nowhere else to be in that small window of time – and who knows where this conversation could lead.

Signs that "now may *not* be the best time" to start a conversation

If you're in a situation and somebody looks miserable, upset or angry then it's pretty obvious that they won't be up for a more general conversation. So avoid people who look down and focus instead on people who have a bit of a smile on their face, a bit of a spring in their step or some energy about them. Pay attention to what they are doing. If they are sitting down with their head in their hands and frantically writing, then that is not the time for you to engage them in idle chitchat.

Likewise, if they are hurrying along in a flustered state and look like they're trying to get somewhere quickly, they are unlikely to be the best person to engage in a conversation.

However, it's not always a total "no go" if someone looks busy. If you really would like to talk to them for a specific reason then there is a way. Watch for when they take a break or come up for air and possibly glance in your direction. At that moment a simple **"Well someone looks busy today"** can work well. Even better, **"Well, someone looks busy today, what are you studying for?"** gets around the risk of a simple smile or a "yes" and is more likely to get them talking. They may not be studying at all but that doesn't matter – they'll probably correct your assumption and give you a route to a conversation.

The Curse of Getting Started

Hesitation kills spontaneity and spontaneity is your friend. Your inner critic will try and stop you, but when you see an opportunity to start a new conversation just go for it. Put aside the urge to critique your opening lines. Just come out with it, straight away, within the first few seconds. If you over-think it, it won't seem natural to you or the person you're connecting with.

Respond to events around you in the environment. If somebody drops something on the floor near you, you could react to it and make a connection with someone else nearby with: **"Glad that wasn't me. That's the sort of thing I do."**

Over-analysis is a short cut to missed opportunities. Don't over-analyze. Another person will accept you if it seems natural to them; and that will only happen if you come across with energy, make good eye contact, and give the impression that you're an open, chatty person.

Aside from responding to events, the most natural moment to engage with somebody is when you move into their physical space.

If you're in a restaurant or coffee shop, the best moment to connect with the person next to you is the very moment you sit down. Use that moment to start your conversation. Moving into someone's physical space creates a natural window. It works because generally you're aware when people move into and out of your space. Think about the last time it happened to you. You probably briefly disengaged with what you were doing to review your surroundings.

If you let your inner critic take over and miss the opportunity, you're left with either having to recreate the moment artificially or resorting to creating or waiting for an event in the environment. Neither of these feels quite as natural.

The real message here is: for the most natural way into a conversation, turn off your inner critic and seize the moment.

6
How – How Do You Mentally and Physically Approach?

How you expect a conversation to go has a huge bearing on how it *actually* goes. It's all about your attitude. You need to be in a good frame of mind and project friendliness and openness. Making a good first impression will determine the quality of the response you get.

Think about your energy levels too. In most cases, before starting a conversation with someone you don't already know it is best to be feeling upbeat and almost spring into action with a question or comment. The energy you have comes across automatically in your tone and body language. If you are feeling a little down it can be difficult to suddenly spring into life. Thinking about something that makes you feel good first is a stepping stone to getting there. Perhaps you could focus on something you're looking forward to or bask in the memory of a recent success. Once you're in the right place mentally, you can "borrow" those positive emotions for the upcoming conversation.

Own Your Environment

When you are surrounded by a group of people you don't know, it's important for you to look to own your environment. Make them aware that you are open to communication and that you are not somebody who is just going to sit quietly in the corner.

Keep in mind it's not just about simply speaking up or what you say. You can also own your environment by taking up more space – so, standing a little wider, perhaps with your legs a bit farther apart, or having your hands on your hips. Also doing things like stretching – stretching your body; stretching your arms and similar movements to make it seem like you are just flexing and loosening up – encourages people to notice you. You take up more space. It's sort of "being seen but not heard" in an unobtrusive way. People who are animated or make sounds come across as being more confident and the proactive leaders in any situation. So, that's why I always say, look to own or at least be a serious contributor to your environment. Otherwise you risk being the quiet wallflower.

An example of owning your environment

A while ago I went into an Apple store because I had a problem with my iPhone. I had an appointment at what they call "The Genius Bar". When I arrived, I was greeted by one of the team members and told to take a seat at one particular table where there were already three other people sitting. Nobody was talking at the table so it seemed like all three people were separate and on their own.

Now, I could have sat there in what would have become a very awkward silence. I decided instead that I would start a conversation and, in doing this, be the talkative one of the table. I made sure I was sitting in a very relaxed manner, with my arms stretched out and leaning across the table, rather than my hands clasped in my lap like the other people at the table. I then simply turned around, moving my head from side to side so that I was making eye contact with all three people and I just said, **"So are you all waiting to see somebody or have any of you been seen?"** Two of them just acknowledged and said, "Waiting" or something similar. One of them started to tell me that she was waiting for somebody to come back to her and that she'd had to back-up her phone before she could have anything else done with it in the store. This then progressed into a conversation between us about what we were there for, what was going on with our iPhones, and so on. But I was the lead person because I had initiated and was asking most of the questions – hence, for want of a better phrase, I was "owning my environment".

Mental: Visualize

Before you speak to someone, imagine the interaction going well. Imagine them *welcoming* your conversation. Visualize it going well and enjoy the thought of the glow you'll feel afterwards from having started the conversation.

Just as important, think about the benefits you're bringing to the other person. You're doing a good thing not a bad thing. Maybe by reaching out you'll:

→ Make them feel good and valued.
→ Add a highlight to their day.
→ Ease an awkward situation or silence.
→ Help them pass a boring moment.

Starting conversations is a good thing for everyone and thinking about it in this way builds your natural enthusiasm. When you are confident that what you are doing is good, you'll embrace it more wholeheartedly and the enthusiasm will come naturally.

People who are best at talking to anyone have developed a supporting belief system. Their belief tells them that starting conversations is fun, valuable and rewarding for everyone. It is like a game to them and an adventure just to see what happens. You need to develop your own belief system to support your goal.

Exercise: Belief System

One way to develop a belief system is through repetition. Make it a habit and repeat the experience again and again. To jump start your new belief system, try this exercise daily for a few weeks.

1. Get into a positive state of mind by thinking about something that excites you or something you're looking forward to.

---

2. Then, using an upbeat tone, repeat over and over, either out loud or in your head:

"Starting conversations is fun; it is a game and an adventure just to see what happens."

3. While saying the words, imagine having fun starting conversations and seeing them going really well in your imagination. Make sure your visualization covers the start and close of a short conversation. See yourself walking away feeling good about the interaction you just had.

4. Repeat several times over a five-minute period.

The important thing to note is that just saying the words won't achieve much. It is when you attach the positive emotion to the words that the magic happens. Combining the mantra with the right emotional state will start to set that belief over time. Do this daily and it will become a new way of thinking – a new habit.

The new belief will be further enforced once you are having these conversations out in the real world.

Mental: The Other Person's Emotional State

You can never know exactly what emotional state anyone is in at any given time. They could be happy, sad, anxious, excited, depressed and so on. There are clues in their body language and posture, but you still can't know exactly what's going through their mind.

It is possible to change someone's emotional state, but it is usually a gradual process rather than an instant switch. If someone looks quiet and withdrawn, leaping at them and being upbeat and happy is just too far away from where they currently are. It's going to aggravate them rather than cheer them up.

What you really need to do is meet them roughly where they are state wise. You need to match them. If you're at, or just slightly above, where they are mentally, then you can move them towards a more positive state.

Matching – using the power of empathy – creates a bridge. The resistance that clashing attitudes creates disappears. The result is rapport, the holy grail of communication. By establishing rapport you can very gradually increase your volume and speed of speech and start to change their emotional state. You can only do this if you've built rapport at their initial state.

Matching emotional states is an essential tool. To some people it comes naturally. If you are not one of them, practise and pay attention to the signs other people are giving off. You can learn to match and build rapport.

Mental: Frames

We all place frames around our communication with others. The "frame" is how you perceive the relationship between you and the other person. For example, you might see them as being superior to you, you superior to them or both of you on an equal footing.

Your attitude, words, tone and body language can be quite different depending on the frame you mentally attach to any situation.

In different situations and frames we talk differently and act differently.

Let's say you are a manager. When you talk to your employees, you probably have a "manager to employee" frame, because you're the boss and they report to you. As soon as you go into the board room to talk to the directors the frame changes. They are the directors, you are the manager. It's a sort of power shift.

But frames are mental constructs, they're not set. So when entering any situation, you can make a choice about the sort of frame you are going to adopt.

How do you adopt a new frame if the default isn't working? When you look at the other person, just imagine somebody else you know with a frame that will work better for you – a good friend perhaps. In most situations a "friends" frame is a good one to adopt for most general day-to-day conversations with people you don't already know.

Visualize the friend clearly in your mind as you look at the other person. See them in the same way you see your friend and imagine this person was present in some of the good times you have spent with your friend. By doing this, you can change the frame and shift your approach, tone and attitude to be more like that of a friend.

Exercise: Framing

→ When you're out and about, look at someone nearby that you don't know.

→ Imagine someone you like standing between the two of you.

→ Look at the person through your imaginary friend.

→ Get into the mental state of that situation and relationship.

→ Notice how your emotional state changes and how your feelings about the person you don't know change.

You can use this technique to transform situations in which you feel intimidated into situations you're comfortable with. With practice it really works.

Physical: How to Physically Approach Someone

Now, you may think the next few sections are common sense, and they are. However, when the pressure of starting a conversation begins to build up, common sense can go out the window. Time and time again I find that clients I am working with who are struggling to start conversations are forgetting one or more of these fundamental rules.

The most important rule about the physical aspects of how you approach someone is: don't approach them from behind. If you do start talking to someone whilst you are behind them, they may not realize you are talking to them or you may startle them. Neither of these is a good start.

Forgetting the obvious

One of my clients wanted to become more confident and social. I taught him many of the things in this book. At a subsequent meeting I asked how things had gone. Badly, he told me; people just didn't want to speak with him. When I asked him to describe the physical positioning of himself and the other person in a specific example, it turned out they were in line in a bank. He was trying to talk to the person in front, who had their back to him. My client assumed that the other person would hear and respond, despite being spoken to from behind. I explained that they may not have heard, they could have been miles away in their own thoughts; or perhaps they didn't want to seem foolish turning round to find out it wasn't them he was talking to. My client could not believe, in this moment of calm review, how he had let all logic and common sense fly out the window during the interaction attempt.

Despite what this example suggests, being directly in front of someone isn't always the ideal position either. You'll probably appear to be blocking their way or cornering them. In certain circumstances though, especially when the other person is standing still, it is all right to be straight in front of someone.

The ideal physical position is to come from side on, i.e. placing yourself to the side of the other person. This could mean you are both facing the same direction or different directions.

You can, however, initiate a conversation with someone behind you quite easily by looking over your shoulder. This is often perceived as a short, casual, non-threatening passing comment in the moment. The other person could be behind you in a line or you may have just walked past them and glance back to say something. If they are walking, aim to talk in motion rather than force them to stop. Forcing someone to stop can be taken as a little pushy and feel awkward.

Not the best way to start a conversation. Once someone has engaged in an ongoing discussion with you it is then OK to stop walking to continue the conversation.

It can also really help the conversation, and acceptance by the other person, if you smile and make good eye contact when speaking to them. Obviously I don't mean an exaggerated glowing smile, which comes across as false. It doesn't have to be a big grin; just a slight smile and holding their attention with good eye contact (without staring) will help make the other person feel more comfortable about the interaction.

Some people find it hard to start smiling. So, another method is to always have a very slight smile on your face – you can practise in the mirror (and you should) so you know what a slight smile feels like!

Physical: Getting Their Attention

One of the biggest problems in starting a conversation with someone you don't know, especially in a general day-to-day public situation, is making sure they know you are actually talking to *them*. Too often people assume the lack of any response means they are being ignored. Many times, though, the other person just doesn't hear or realize that they are the one being spoken to, just like the example of my client in the bank.

This is why making sure you are in the line of sight of someone you wish to engage with and making eye contact with a brief smile are important – they let that person know you are speaking to them.

If necessary you can get their attention by starting with a slightly louder voice than you would normally use and simply say "Excuse me", pausing (to give them time to engage) before continuing with what you were going to say. This is more suitable for instances, like standing behind someone, where you are not easily visible to them. If, however, you are in a shop beside someone else looking at the same shelves, you can take a different approach and simply say your whole opening gambit without a pause. It is important to make sure you are standing close enough and turned towards them slightly, and perhaps even lean towards them slightly, so they have no doubt you are talking to them.

A few ways to get somebody's attention: If, in the shop example, you were going to ask for help or advice, you could use **"Excuse me"** at the start. For example:

"Excuse me; you wouldn't happen to know which of these puzzles is best for a 10-year-old boy would you?"

However, if you were just making a passing throwaway comment you would not.

"There are just too many great things here to choose from; I could be here all day."

Another way to get people's attention, and perhaps even have them start a conversation with you, is to wear something unusual that could be commented on. Although in this case you are not deciding who to talk to – they are selecting you. You could, however, make this work for you if you used the unusual item to start a conversation by asking someone else's opinion on it. For example, suppose you had a very colourful watch on that looked like it could be a child's watch. You could use this to your advantage by asking people something like:

"Excuse me, could I get your opinion on something? My friends say I shouldn't wear this watch as it looks like a 5-year-old's watch, but I think it's fun, what do you think?"

In any situation, once you have the idea or inclination to speak to someone you should do so immediately or within five seconds. Otherwise doubts and inner talk can start to put you off.

Just doing it as it comes to mind is the key.

Physical: Opening Styles

Different situations call for adopting different opening styles: submissive, neutral or dominant. There is no value judgement in these labels – dominant doesn't mean aggressive, it just means authoritative. Likewise, submissive doesn't mean weak. All three are valuable strategies that you need to learn to use depending on the situation.

Let's say you need to ask for directions from somebody in the street. Many people in this situation would go very submissive, apologetic and quiet with:

> "Oh excuse me I wonder . . . I don't know if you could tell me the way to the museum could you?"

The chances are that even if the person you ask knows the way they will likely ignore you. They may say "Sorry I don't know" or they may not even hear the question. Basically they are unlikely to feel compelled to stop and engage with you.

A dominant approach is unlikely to work either. You can't really say in a stern voice:

> "Can you tell me the way to the museum?"

You'll probably be ignored or get a "No, sorry" response.

A good strategy in this situation is to start out dominant and then switch to submissive. So **"Excuse me"** would be said reasonably loud to get attention, but once you have the person engaged, the rest of the sentence switches to submissive: **"You wouldn't happen to know the way to the museum would you?"** A dominant opening can cause brief concern that something may be wrong, so when followed by a more submissive tone, the sense of relief often means that the other person is only too pleased to help!

In every situation, you need to ask yourself what mode is appropriate for the outcome you want. And remember – how you start doesn't have to be how you carry on (although it is easier to change down from dominant to a more submissive level than it is to go up a level).

One More Thing

Talking to new people takes time and practice. We get better over time, but most people experience the really strange phenomenon where they can feel like they've cracked it one day, and the next it's all gone. It almost seems like yesterday didn't happen and it becomes awkward again. One such viewpoint goes back to prehistoric times. In the early caveman days humans lived in tribes, which may have consisted of a limited number of people – perhaps thirty to seventy. Back in those times, venturing outside of your own tribe and coming across another was considered a risk of being killed.

Given this, and how the human brain has evolved over time, an element of this natural caveman instinct is believed to still exist in the deepest parts of our brains. This might explain the reason why many people seem to make great progress on a particular day at speaking to strangers, but find it difficult to do so again the next day. For many people this is normal. It is almost as if we are reset to old behaviours overnight.

There is a way to really help this and that is to start every day being very social with people that are quite easy to talk to. For example, this could be the person at the station where you buy your ticket, the taxi driver, the shopkeeper or the bus driver. People tend to find that by the time they have had three "warm up" conversations at the start of the day, all other conversations are much easier.

So, instead of paying for your petrol or newspaper and just saying "Thank you", ask a question or pass a comment – engage the other person in a brief conversation.

Sometimes these interactions may develop into conversations; other times they will not. The outcome or amount of conversation that takes place isn't important. The point is you are developing your conversation-starting skills and making progress all the time. Like most things, the more practice you have the more you improve.

7
What – What Do You Say?

Obviously one of the most crucial aspects of starting a conversation is your opening – the question or statement that you initially make to start a conversation.

With fear reduced or out of the way, the next common barrier that people have is what to *say* to start a conversation. We've already explored some environmental and other situation-based openings. Now let's look at openings in general and how, once you have started with an opening, you can engage the other person further and spot the signs that they are engaged in your conversation.

Types of Opening Statements

The first thing that is said in any communication is called the opening. There are a number of different ways to open a conversation:

→ Situational.
→ Observational.

→ Opinion/advice.

→ Assistance.

A **situational opening** is where you say something based on the situation that you and the other person are both in: at a sporting event; at a business seminar; at a party. You open with something that relates to your current shared experience.

An **observational opening** is also based on shared experience – this time, of an event or incident. It could be something you are doing, wearing or something in the shared environment. For instance, let's say you've just gone into a shop and outside there was an argument going on between two people. An observational statement could be along the lines of **"Did you see those two out there? It was getting pretty frantic."**

Opinion/advice openings are closely related. In this scenario, your opener is designed to solicit a response that will be helpful to you. Often an **opinion opening** is best started by saying something along the lines of, **"Excuse me, could I get a quick opinion on something, please?"** The trick here is to flow straight into the opinion you are looking for without waiting for them to respond. So, for example, **"Excuse me, could I get your quick opinion on something, please? Do you think . . . "** An **advice opening** achieves the same result, but tends to add a directional layer; you are asking what the other person thinks you should do. This can be very flattering!

When you see someone who needs help, an **assistance opening** is a great way to begin communication with them. Let's say you are in a tourist area in a city and there are lots of people taking photographs, you could simply offer to take a picture of a group with their camera.

You may see someone struggling to get shopping into their car and offer to help; this is another example of where you could initiate a conversation by offering assistance.

Pace Their Reality or Meet Them Where They Are!

One of the best ways to make people feel more comfortable about your communication with them is to "pace their reality". This means you meet them where they are and include a statement about what they are currently doing in your opening comment. On a subconscious level this basically makes the conversation or communication more relevant, and real, because the other person agrees exactly with what you said.

For example, if you see somebody sitting, reading a book, you would open with, **"I noticed you there reading that book and couldn't help wonder . . . "** . In this case, you have paced their reality. Another example would be, **"While you are standing there waiting, you wouldn't mind if I just asked your opinion on something, would you?"** or **"While I see you standing there, you couldn't answer a quick question for me, could you?"** In this case, we have seen somebody who is standing, waiting, perhaps for a bus or a train or to get into somewhere, and we have paced their reality.

Pacing their reality is very important and it really is simple. It basically consists of just stating what they are doing or currently experiencing. They will agree with what you have started to say because you have stated some facts very relevant to them – hence a level of rapport is established immediately.

Spot the Start of Their Engagement

Once the conversation gets going or you at least get past your opening statement, what you then need to look out for is the start of the other person's engagement. This is when they have started to engage in the communication and you have moved them away from one-word answers. Once you have spotted engagement you know the other person is relaxed and you have something to build the conversation on. It is at this point where the two of you are in rapport. Some conversations will reach engagement quickly; others will take a little while. Of course some may never engage, and that is fine. We were merely giving them an opportunity.

Typical signs that the other person has started to engage or is engaged in your conversation would include:

→ Nodding.
→ Smiling.
→ Laughing.
→ Making good eye contact.
→ Giving longer answers to your questions.
→ Going into more detail when they answer you, rather than just trying to get away with a quick yes, no or one- or two-word answer.
→ Moving closer to you or even leaning in a bit.
→ Starting to ask you questions.

Once the other person starts fully contributing to the communication – asking you questions, adding their own comment and giving you more back than you have actually asked for – that is when you know that person is engaged in the communication and you have built rapport.

Engaging people who are resistant

When you want to get resistant people engaged (they could be shy, or just not really engaging), avoid asking endless questions. Mix in some statements between questions, for example:

> YOU: "That looks like my sort of cookery book – meals in 15 minutes, does it work?" [QUESTION]

> THEM: "Yes." [SHORT ANSWER NO ENGAGE-MENT]

> YOU: "My friend says that any meal that takes less than an hour to cook isn't worth eating, the best meals take time." [STATEMENT]

They may reply to this as it is a tempting statement that they could give an opinion on, if not you could ask something along these lines:

> YOU: "So what's the longest time you've taken to cook a meal and was it the best meal ever?"

This works on a couple of levels. Firstly, we are putting out a tempting statement they may have an opinion on and, secondly, we are asking a couple of questions that they really have to engage in to answer. What's more, these questions are not challenging or prying, and the other person should be comfortable giving more than a one-word answer.

Keep It Simple with People You've Never Met Before

To avoid making people you have just met for the first time feel awkward, it is a good idea to ask questions they will know the answer to. It is also important to focus on things they are likely to be happy to speak about. For example, once a conversation has been started, a tourist could be asked about where they live and how it compares. They could feel uncomfortable if you ask a question they don't know the answer to or one that is too specific or personal too soon in the conversation.

Most of the scenarios I am describing are around one-to-one conversations. However, with a group of people who are obviously together you can approach with something like **"Looks like this is the area here where it is all happening"** – the actual words of course will depend on the situation and venue. This works well in a social environment like a pub or bar and could continue with something like **"So, how do you all know each other?"**

Remain aware of how people respond to you. If you make sensible comments and they reply in a humorous way, then look to continue the conversation with a more humorous approach. On the other hand, if you start with humour but get a serious reply, then you should take a more serious approach until rapport is built.

Topic Hints and Conversation Hijacking

It goes without saying that the best topics to engage someone with are the topics that they want to talk about. So how can you work this out?

There are clues to the topics that people are keen to talk about in what they say. For instance, let's say you ask a work colleague or a friend how their weekend was. They said, "We had a brilliant weekend. We went to the cinema." At this point we have reached a major decision point in the communication. If you want to build rapport and carry the conversation deeper with this person, you should ask them questions about their experience of going to the cinema, to encourage them to engage with you about it. For instance, you may ask them what their favourite film is of all time or **"How busy was the cinema?"** – any number of questions that you could ask about their experience, which, as we know, was something they enjoyed doing this weekend.

The mistake that a lot of people make in this exact situation is immediately turning the conversation back to themselves. Instead of asking how the other person's experience was at the cinema, they might say: "Well, I went to football and it was really funny at football. I'll tell you what happened . . ." They've diverted the topic of conversation from being about the other person's good experience at the cinema and turned it into their own experience of going to football! The other person may well have no interest in that topic at all. Even if they do have an interest in football, they're going to be far less interested in talking to you about your weekend than their weekend, where we first started out. The conversation has been hijacked!

So, make sure that you are always trying to draw topics from what the other person is offering in their communication and words; asking them more questions or giving opinions or statements on what they have told you. Once rapport and engagement is built though, and you've spotted engagement, then you can start to change the topic and take the conversation where *you* want it to go.

Avoid Classic Chitchat for too Long

In all communications and conversations you want to avoid classic chitchat for too long – things like talking about the weather and other day-to-day, general matters. Get onto topics that the other person enjoys talking about as quickly as possible. Find their hotspots and ask about them. Get them to relive those experiences and tell you about them. Real and meaningful connection occurs once you get away from chitchat – once you get that lock-in of engagement.

I now want to share with you one of the most amazing openings of all time. This is an opening that you can use pretty much anywhere, in any situation, with anyone – it's your "get out of jail free card" when you are stuck for something to say: it involves you being a little creative (i.e. not being totally honest) but no one suffers from it!

The fantastic opening that can be used anywhere with anyone is quite simply this:

"Was it you I was talking to earlier in here?"

Now it's a little bit cheeky because you know you weren't talking to that person earlier. However, what you are doing, or trying to appear to be doing, is making a genuine identification mistake in that, for whatever reason, you thought this was somebody you were talking to earlier that day or that week. This is something you can use for opening a conversation when you are really stuck and you can't think of anything else to say in that situation to get it going. So, for instance, just simply saying, **"Hi there. Was it you I was talking to earlier about websites and developing websites?"**

They'll obviously say, "No." You then reply **"Oh, really? Well, you look a lot like this person I was talking to earlier this week when we got onto the subject of what they do and websites. Are you sure you haven't got a twin brother?"** – to which they may answer yes or no and you could continue a conversation. In any case, you could just follow up with, **"Oh, I'm really, really sorry. You must have a double walking around. So what are you doing here?"** – and lead into another conversation, perhaps about making mistakes like this! It's just a really good way, when you're stuck for what to say, to open a conversation with someone new you'd really like to talk to, without resorting to the normal weather-based chitchat.

Is it all about the opening? Well, yes and no. Conversations cannot start without an opening. However, it doesn't always matter what you open with topic wise because quite often you can take the conversation absolutely anywhere once you have initial engagement from the other person. For instance, say you saw someone you'd like to talk to about a business opportunity. The trouble is in the moment you are not sure how to start talking about it to this person. It's perfectly OK to start the conversation with a general matter first – such as an observational opening. You can then build a connection and engagement, and bring the business topic in later.

So, now you understand the different types of openings and how to use them to get started. You also know how to spot the signs that the other person has started to engage in the conversation, as well as how to help this happen faster. We have also explored one of the most fundamental rules of communication – to avoid "hijacking" the conversation and spend more time on topics that other people are interested in.

Let's now discover how to create even more engagement by getting the other person really interested and/or curious about the topic of our conversation or where we are hoping to take the conversation.

8
Stage 2 – Creating Curiosity and Interest

In your conversations with people, one of your key objectives is to keep their attention. Only when their attention is locked into your conversation do you stand a chance of building rapport and taking things where you'd like them to go. The best way to keep someone's attention is to generate their curiosity or interest in what you are saying. Curiosity and interest can, of course, be built through the tonality that we use, but one of the best ways to do this is by talking in terms of either stories or interesting facts. Also, talking about unusual facts that are relevant to the situation can engage people more and help to create that element of curiosity and interest in what you are saying.

Leading Their Imagination

Language directs our thinking. By just changing a word or two in a phrase, the response we get and the mental journey we send people on can be completely different. Let's look at a phrase around somebody winning the lottery. You could ask someone **"What would you do if you won the lottery?"** This is likely to get them thinking about all of the things that they would buy with the money if they were to win.

However, there is a good chance that asking a slightly different question – **"What would winning the lottery do for you?"** – will get the person thinking about different things; about what it would mean to them and their lives in general, as opposed to specific things they might buy. This could be things like, "I wouldn't have to worry about all the bills to pay, I'd have peace of mind, I'd have the freedom to do what I'd like to do."

So, as you see, by thinking carefully about how we phrase our questions, we can direct the other person's thinking along the lines that we'd like them to go. The use of words leads the imagination and it is through the imagination that we can build fantastic relationships with other people.

Phrases such as **"Did you know that . . . ?"** or **"I wonder if you've ever heard this, but . . . "** are all lead-ins to what should be a curiosity- or interest-raising question or statement.

Opening with the simple phrase **"If you were to . . . "** or **"When you think about . . . "** also encourages people to open up their imagination to what you are about to tell them. For example, **"If you were to go on a Caribbean holiday for a month, what would you do every day?"**

This tells the other person that they need to imagine what you are about to tell them in order to make sense of the statement. In doing this, of course, we know the sort of things the other person will be imagining and, out of that, we will have a pretty good idea whether they are going to be thinking about good things or bad things. So, this means that, through the power of our words, we are not only leading the other person's imagination but we can also lead the direction of their emotional state.

The Power of Stories

When the other person fully understands what you are saying and appreciates what you are telling them, then rapport exists at another level. People don't like to be in a situation where they don't understand things or where they can't quite make sense of what someone else is saying to them. This is why stories are fantastic. When you can get your point across through a story, or a worked example, then the other person is much more likely to fully understand the points you want to convey. Stories create better understanding and build rapid rapport. As soon as we start hearing a story from somebody, we engage a lot more. We have grown up loving and listening to stories as children; wondering where they are going and how they are going to work out.

A good friend of mine once told me, after one of my conference talks, "The brilliant thing about you, Mark, is you tell such fantastic stories in all of your topics." I replied that I didn't tell any stories. I merely told people what I knew. My friend replied to me with some examples of stories he had heard me recount through the evening. I realized at this point that what I thought were worked examples – ways of getting my point across and encouraging the audience to understand what I meant – were, in fact, stories. It was then

I understood that stories are also a fantastic way of getting your point across in conversations.

Let's take an example to see why this works.

While I was out with a client he asked me about this very book, that you are reading right now. I told him it was about how to talk to absolutely anyone and how anyone could quite easily engage people they didn't know in conversations. He didn't believe it. He said, "You cannot go and talk to someone you don't know". At the time, we were in a restaurant. It was a restaurant where you went up, placed your order and then went and sat at your table.

We had finished our sandwiches and I wanted to get some more food so I said to him, "I'll go up to place another order and while I'm there, I'll talk to a complete stranger so that you can see it is totally possible". Whilst I was waiting in line, a lady came into the restaurant and stood behind me in the queue. I turned around to glance in her direction, only to realize she was busy typing into her phone. This wasn't the ideal time to start a conversation. She was obviously engrossed in something and me starting a conversation at that point would be interrupting her and probably not going to get the best response. So I waited a while. Having paid for my food, I was waiting for my order to arrive when the lady's turn came to pay. She actually waved her phone in front of the checkout till to scan something on her phone to make payment.

She then came and stood next to me to wait for her order, at which point I simply said, **"Wow. That was impressive – paying for your order like that. Certainly showed me up, fumbling around in my pockets for loose change!"** She laughed and then went on to explain how it was a great facility but she didn't really keep track of everything she was spending. This meant that her lunch bill at the end of the month would be much larger than it used to be. We chatted some more about technology. She started asking me some questions and, therefore, I spotted that she was locked-in and engaged in the conversation. When my order arrived, I collected my food and said to her, "Great to meet you. See you later" and she said to me, "Great to meet you too. Have a great day." She wasn't upset that I started a conversation with her because it came across as genuine and interesting. It was an observational opening based on something that she was doing, which then opened up the opportunity to speak about a number of other similar topics.

My client was amazed.

What did you learn? As well as being an interesting tale in itself, the story actually contained many different lessons: including when to engage and when not to engage with someone, how to start the conversation and how to spot the signs of engagement, and leaving it on a good note. If the example had simply listed the lessons instead of telling you the story, the points being made about starting a conversation may not have resonated as well.

You can lead into a story, if its purpose is to get a point across, by simply saying, **"For instance . . . "** or **"Let's say something happened like this . . . "** Stories also give us the opportunity to pull the person we are talking to into the story. Very often, when we hear a story we associate more with one character or role in that story than another. So, when you are telling a story and you want the other person to be sympathetic about you and your role in the story – if that is what is appropriate at that point in time – you can do that through the way you tell the story, perhaps even starting with the statement **"How would you feel if this had happened to you? Let me tell you exactly what happened."**

Stories also enable you to impart and share a lot of information and experience within a short period of time. Simultaneously, rapport is built yet again because the person listening to the story will very often associate what you have told them with an experience they have had or somebody else they know has had, or that they observed. As soon as these common ground areas are found, a bond and a connection are made at another level.

Be a great conversationalist – through use of stories

Another great advantage of telling stories is that you come across as a great conversationalist, because you are recounting something that you already know from memory. You are not creating a story on the fly (unless, of course, you are lying). So, when you tell a genuine story, you are simply describing exactly what happened. You've got that movie in your mind so your conversation just flows and absorbs the other person in it. Compare this to striking up a conversation and not quite knowing where it's going. You stumble, stutter and think about your next word. So it's always far easier to tell a story.

At networking events, for instance, a lot of people struggle when they have to stand up and speak for a minute about their business and the sort of business they are looking for. Very often they will prepare a script to recite. However, when it comes to the one-minute presentation, they very often stumble and make mistakes or forget their way when reading the script.

So, I always say to people, "If speaking isn't your thing and you've got to do a presentation, why not do it in the context of a story?" Just stand up for a minute and tell people about a particular customer that you dealt with this week or a particular project that you have been involved in recently. Just simply tell it as a story – "This is what they came to us for. This is what we did. These are the problems we solved and this is how we left them afterwards and that's what we can do for everybody else. So who do you know like the person in my story that I could help as well?"

Stories make things interesting and stories make things simple. They are also an opportunity to let people get to know the real you. A story about an experience you have had in your life, growing up or even a trauma you went through or a fantastic victory that you achieved helps the other person fully understand more about you, your values and your beliefs.

Your attitude affects the outcome you get

Perhaps the best way to illustrate the power of a story, then, is to tell you a story. So, instead of simply saying that your attitude and approach greatly affect the outcome of your communication, I will replace that with a true story.

I went into a coffee shop to get some coffee and catch up on some work before an important meeting. To secure my table, I put my jacket and rucksack over a couple of the chairs.

As I ordered my coffee, I heard a commotion break out. As I looked back down the store, I could see that a homeless person had just been given a cup of water by a member of staff. However, it seemed that a businessman had come into the shop just as the homeless person was leaving and there had been some sort of argument between them. This argument, based on what was being said, was centred around how the businessman had looked at the homeless person with a level of disapproval. The homeless person then decided to take a seat at one of the tables instead of leaving. As he did this, two ladies sitting at a table nearby got up and moved away. This infuriated him even further and more torrents of abuse and bad language flowed from his mouth.

The problem I was suddenly faced with was that this very angry person was now sitting at the table next to the one that I had reserved! In fact, his arm was leaning on my table. "What do I do?" I thought. "If I go and move my jacket and bag to go somewhere else he's going to go completely mad. But do I really want to go and sit there with him while he is in that mood? Oh, I'm saved," I thought, as one coffee shop employee went over to talk to him – and then the abuse and language rose to a whole new level. The homeless person was shouting in the face of the coffee shop worker, "Get out of my face! I will leave here when I am ready. You will regret it if you don't get out of my face now!" It seemed that the member of staff had gone over and asked him quietly to leave, but this was instead taken as an insult and a form of discrimination. The staff member then returned to his post, leaving me with my dilemma.

Then it occurred to me – this guy obviously had some things going on in his life that had led him to where he is today. Therefore, perhaps I should be curious. He would probably prefer not to be in that situation, but to be living a life more similar to the rest of us in the coffee shop. So, I decided, "What if I was to think of him as a friend and just go over, sit down at my table with my cake and with my coffee and engage him in conversation?"

As I began to walk towards my seat, he began to glare in my direction. The closer I got, the angrier he seemed to get. But as I got to the table, I looked at him, made eye contact, smiled slightly and simply said, **"Hi there. How's it all going then?"** He looked at me and then started to ask me some questions, which were quite unusual. Then he began to tell me some of his life story. I maintained eye contact. I smiled at different points. We engaged in conversation about the price of sandwiches in coffee shops. And in the end, he got up to leave, asked me my name, told me his name and shook my hand before going on his way.

If the staff member had gone over and sat with him for a minute or two, built some rapport and then asked him if he'd mind leaving, the outcome of the conversation would probably have been completely different. The person working in the coffee shop would have achieved the outcome he wanted and avoided the torrent of bad language, abuse and threats, simply by pacing the reality of the homeless person – engaging him in some meaningful, friendly conversation to build rapport and then moving the conversation on afterwards.

So, by being careful about the words we use, we can better capture the imagination of the people we are talking to. As a result, they become more engaged with us and very often want to find out more, or share more information with us. Stories are an excellent way to capture the other person's imagination and at the same time make it easy for you to lead the conversation. What's more, you look like a skilled conversationalist when reciting a story.

Now we need to further develop the connection with the person we are talking to and, at the same time, make sure they feel like they are being understood. After all, no one wants to talk with someone who doesn't, or they think doesn't, understand them.

9
Stage 3 – Making a Connection and Being Understood

In order to really move things forward and get somebody onboard with your point of view, or to take a conversation to where you want it to go, that person needs to feel that they are like you to some degree and that you have the same values or are thinking along the same lines. They need to feel that you have a vested interest together. You achieve all of this when you make a connection with someone and you are certain that you are being understood. In this chapter, we will look at how to achieve this. We'll look at language, the key words that people use and even how the speed at which you talk can affect building a connection and being understood. We do all this to ensure, as much as we can, that we are on track to getting people onboard with where we want to go. Sometimes great communication can be all about getting the other person to come up with your ideas!

There is a common saying when people talk about property or selling houses: "location, location, location" – meaning, of course, that location is the most important thing to consider. We have a similar saying with regards to communication: "listen, listen, listen". Communication is more about listening than the words being said. When you listen, pay attention and understand the other person, and ask them for clarification on areas that don't seem obvious to you, you build a greater understanding of what they really mean; then, with very few words you can reply to them and have a fantastic outcome to your conversation.

A great way to build a connection and get the other person to open up more is by asking questions like:

→ **"How did you do that?"**
→ **"Why did you do that?"**
→ **"How did it make you feel?"**

In order to really engage in the conversation with someone, and gain a position where you can come back with very relevant questions or comments, actually imagine yourself being in whatever situation they are in or the situation they are describing to you. In this way, you get to live a little bit of their experience and can then gather valuable insights to enable you to come up with great responses, such that they will want to tell you even more. As we have already discovered in Chapter 8, it is really important for you, whenever possible, to communicate in stories rather than facts. Obviously it depends on the topic of conversation but, generally, when you want to build understanding, a story is worth a thousand facts.

What you do want to avoid though, is asking too many questions of somebody else. If you get into this situation, then it can seem more like an interrogation and the conversation never really starts to flow. It's all one-sided. Once you get the conversation flowing, then common points of interest or connection start to occur. The more you can find out about somebody, the more chances there are that common points of interest are going to come up, and that is when the connection happens – you feel alike – and the relationship immediately moves to another level.

Being Understood – An Example

I heard somebody tell a story once about the importance of being understood, and it has stuck with me ever since. During a survey in the United States of America, interviewers stood outside a large store speaking to those customers who came out having engaged in conversation with a sales assistant but not purchased anything. They reported that 90% of the shoppers who had engaged with a sales person but not gone on to purchase anything said a very similar thing: "They didn't understand what I was looking for" or "They didn't understand what I needed and just kept offering me things that were not suitable". You see – in this situation the shoppers did not feel understood. They didn't feel as if the shop assistant really understood what it was they were looking for or what was important to them about the particular product they were looking to purchase.

"What's Important to You?"

As you have just discovered, you really need to find out in most circumstances what is important to the other person. So, if you are talking to somebody and they are asking for help or guidance, you need to find out what is important to them. If someone asks you for a film or holiday destination recommendation, simply coming out with things that you like or enjoy may not be relevant to them and they could perceive you as somebody who gives poor advice. However, if you first take a step back and say to them, **"More than happy to help with some advice on a holiday destination. Could I just ask you though, what is important to you about a holiday?"** they will then begin to tell you all of the attributes of a holiday that are important to them. For instance, if they enjoy a quiet, relaxing holiday where there isn't very much to do, but you enjoy a very active holiday, then the recommendations you may have made, if you didn't know what was important to them, would not be appropriate. This is why finding out what is important to the other person is so "important"!

Here is an example of this in action that I recently experienced while doing some one-to-one mentoring with two managers in an organization. In the first staff member's mentoring session, I said to him, **"Could I ask you about careers – what's most important to you about your career and work life?"** He replied, "Knowledge. Knowledge is most important because with knowledge, the world is your oyster. You can do whatever you want and you can make things happen." When it came to the mentoring session with the second manager and I asked him the same question, he said, "Money. Money is most important. With money, you can have the freedom to do whatever you want."

Now, knowing this meant that I could take those conversations on further, focusing around the areas that were most important to them.

Knowing what is important to individuals is very valuable in any situation. For example, if I were looking to market a seminar for people to attend, then knowing what's most important to them greatly helps me target my marketing message to the individuals concerned. If I was going to do a training workshop on how to have a winning mindset and be successful, I would say to the first employee that if he attended my seminar he would have more *knowledge* about what it takes to live a successful life and have a successful mindset than 99% of the world's population. I would tell the second employee that if he attended the same workshop he would learn skills and techniques with the potential to give him the power of *earning more* in a month than he currently earns in a year.

Now both of these statements are true. I am not misleading anyone, because the training workshop could achieve either of these objectives.

Making it Easier for People to Understand What You're Saying

So how do you make people feel you are more like them? How can you make it easier for them to understand what you are saying and to feel understood? One of the interesting things about the way our minds work is that we all tend to process information in different ways. When we understand how others process information, we can use this to connect and engage with them in a way that works for them.

We often change the way we process information, depending on the circumstances we are in. Sometimes we process information visually, thinking about things by making pictures in our minds. We might imagine what a scene would look like or imagine ourselves being in a particular scene. Other times our thinking may be generated from an auditory perspective. We might talk to ourselves in our head, using our inner voice to think things through. We may even remember things other people have said, or imagine what they might say. On other occasions our thinking may be generated from a feelings or kinaesthetic perspective.

These visual, auditory and kinaesthetic ways of processing information are called "representational systems" in NLP. In other words, it's how we represent an inner experience to ourselves in order to process and understand it and, where appropriate, provide a given response. The thing to bear in mind is that most of us process information through all three perspectives all of the time. In any given context, though, one of these will be our main way of thinking at any specific point in time.

Generally, the words someone is using – the representational language – demonstrate how or in what mode that person is currently thinking. Someone who is mainly thinking in pictures and imagining scenes is likely to say something like "I *see* what you mean" or "That will *look* good". Somebody using their inner voice or remembering things other people have said is more likely to say something like, "That *sounds* like a good idea", "That *sounds* like something I could be involved in" or "I *hear* what you say". However, someone who is coming from a feelings or kinaesthetic perspective is more likely to say things like "Well, that *feels* like the right sort of direction to go in" or "I just need to try and *get a grip* on things and then I'll be able to move forward". Can you see how the words and phrases used are all centred around whether they are coming from a visual, auditory or feelings/kinaesthetic perspective?

How fast do you talk?

Another interesting aspect of this way of processing and thinking – that determines the language and words we typically use in conversation – is that it also tends to affect how fast we speak.

Very often you will find that somebody who is thinking visually – making pictures in their head – will speak quite quickly. Perhaps this has something to do with the saying "A picture paints a thousand words" and for every picture they see in their heads, they have to get a thousand words out!

People who think in an auditory way – perhaps using self-talk or things they remember other people saying or imagining what somebody else might say, for instance – tend to talk a little bit slower because they have to listen to the voice or imagine the voice before they respond.

Finally, someone who is coming more from a feelings or kinaesthetic perspective is likely to speak much slower again. They have to feel every experience so that they can process it before they respond with their comment or question to add to the conversation.

So how does this help us? Well, if somebody says to you, "Well, that *looks* like something that could work", you could reply with **"Well, if that *looks* good, you're going to love it when you see this"**. Here, you've continued talking from a visual perspective and, hence, stand more chance of building the connection and keeping rapport. If, instead, you had said, "Well, if you like that, wait until you *hear* about this", you'd have moved this from their visual perspective to your auditory perspective.

We do this all the time in everyday life, so don't worry about it too much with regard to not speaking along the same lines as another person. If you really want to take that connection or that level of understanding to the next tier though, then this is a great way to do this. It's another building block in the process of building rapport with the other person and making it easier for them to understand what you are saying.

What Words Are They Using?

Rapport can also be built by using key words that are appropriate to the person you are talking to. This is important because, for instance, in different cultures and different countries, different words are used to describe the same things. When you use a different word that somebody is not used to in a conversation, it does momentarily cause a gap in rapport, exposing a difference between the two of you. For example, in America people would talk about an "elevator" whereas in the UK the same thing would be called a "lift". In America they have "parking lots" but in the UK we have "car parks".

So, whenever I was working with American companies or having conversations with American companies, I would make sure I would use their words as much as possible. I would call it a "parking lot". I would call it an "elevator". It's an easy thing for me to do and it helps build rapport further because there is less internal processing for the other person to do. In the case of the parking lot, if I were saying "car park" the other person has to either ask me what that is or make that internal conversion themselves and say, "Oh yes, they mean 'parking lot', don't they? They call it something different in the UK."

You can attempt to match the "key criteria" words that other people use to describe an experience. If somebody says, "I had a fantastic holiday", then a key criteria word for them there is the word "fantastic". If I want to continue that conversation and keep the rapport really, really tight, I should say something like **"That sounds good. In which ways was your holiday fantastic?"** because the word "fantastic" has real meaning for them in the experience they are describing to me. If you use different key criteria words, such as "brilliant" instead of "fantastic" in this example, you risk disconnecting the other person from their own experience or memory. This could be useful in some ways if you wanted to move somebody away from an experience. For example, if someone was stuck and kept saying things were "impossible", you might reply to them that perhaps they were just "challenging" and needed a different approach. Rephrasing the key criteria word to "challenging" from "impossible" creates a greater chance they will look for a solution to their issue. They become open to the possibility of a solution. However, in general, if you want to build rapport and keep them engaged in the experience, you need to match those key criteria words. Now, I'm not talking about you becoming a parrot and simply repeating everything other people say. Just make yourself aware of these sorts of words, so that you can use them when responding to something they have just told you.

Be careful of the fact that, although two words might sound similar to you, they may have very different meanings to the person you are talking to. For instance, the other person may say that they'd like a challenge – where their interpretation of the word "challenge" means something that they would have a go at and look to overcome any obstacles in order to achieve success in. However, they may associate the word "challenging" with something different, perhaps seeing this as something that they are unable to do and will struggle with. So, if somebody says, "I like a good challenge" and you reply, "Well, you may well find this *challenging*", it might not connect on the same level as it would if you had said, **"Well, I know something that you would also find an interesting challenge"**.

Another situation in which to make use of key criteria words is when you know what people are passionate about – their hobbies, interests and the things they enjoy doing. These hobbies and interests have words associated with them and it is very likely that those words remind a person of their hobby or passion – hence, they have a good association and a good feeling about those words.

I had a client once who loved flying. He had his own glider that he would take out pretty much every weekend and on a Monday we would hear about the latest flight he had undertaken. Now there are many words associated with flying that are used in everyday language. However, using these words in association with something I was aiming for this client to do, such as sign me up for another project, generated a better feeling or state within my client. After all, he is more likely to agree to something if he is in a really good mood!

So, for example, as he had this hobby, I could quite easily say about a potential project **"Hey, I think we should do this because if we implement this new project, I think things could really *take off*. In fact, I reckon that when we get this going and things are underway, *the sky is the limit*."** Now phrases like "the sky is the limit" or "take off" are commonly used within the field of gliding and will remind someone of the experience, if it is something they are into. Every time I was able to get his mind to briefly glimpse his experience of gliding, he was going to experience an element of good feeling about it. And what do I want him to have regarding my project? A good feeling. This is the power of using key criteria words in your conversations with people.

Decision Strategies

I have already covered the area of finding out what is important to people. Another great thing about asking people what's important to them is that it tells us what their strategy is for making a decision. For everything that we do in life, we have a strategy, a way of thinking about things or making decisions. Knowing someone's decision strategy for a given circumstance will help you redirect the conversation towards things that match their particular strategy. So, for instance, when talking to somebody about buying a television, if you ask what's important to them about a television or what they look for in a television, they are going to reply with their buying-decision strategy. They may tell you about the style, the size, the make and the colour – features that are important to them. This then means you can preselect particular televisions that match their criteria before replying with what you could offer them by way of a television. They are far more likely to say yes to one of your televisions because you have presented them with only relevant ones. Had you offered up options outside of their criteria, you could have caused confusion, the feeling that you don't understand what they really need, resulting in them going away "to think about it".

Most people in sales would probably say "So what sort of television are you looking for?" This probably won't get as detailed and useful an answer as **"Could I ask you what is most important to you about the television you get?"**

This isn't just restricted to business life, of course; it can be used in your everyday social life as well. For instance, very often I like to go out at weekends and look at cars for sale. My wife wouldn't see this as a very exciting trip out on a Sunday afternoon. However, what I *do* know is that she enjoys it when we go for a drive in the country and perhaps stop off and get a coffee somewhere. I can use this knowledge to get her onboard with the idea of going out and looking at cars by simply saying, **"Hey, why don't we go out for a drive in the country? We could grab a coffee, have a nice little drive around and perhaps while we are out, I might just pop in to a car dealer showroom as well. What do you think?"** I am more likely to get a yes to that suggestion than to "Hey, why don't we go out and have a look around some car dealers this afternoon?" There is nothing in that statement that matches anything my wife would like to do or that is important to her.

Once you know what's important to people, and you know their strategy for making decisions in a given situation, you can use that to help influence the results you get from your conversations and communication.

This isn't about coercing people or forcing people against their will to do anything. What you are doing is pointing out that, in most cases, the things that you would like to do contain elements of what they like as well. You highlight the things that they like so they can see there are benefits for them as well.

Dealing with Questions

In life, we are often asked questions by other people during our conversations. In fact, the whole conversation may start with a question that somebody wants to ask us. Now, through our lives, we tend to grow up expecting, on one level or another, that very often when we ask a question, we won't actually get an answer. People, in fact, frequently sidestep our questions and answer about something completely different. This is something you may have noticed in particular with politicians where, when faced with a question they don't want to answer, they in fact give an answer to a different question altogether, very often trying to make it appear relevant and applicable.

In order to get the other person to pay attention to your answers, and really appreciate from the very start that you are addressing their question, it is best to include their initial question at the beginning of your answer. If someone said to you "What would I need to do in order to get a promotion at work?" – assuming this is one of your own team members, of course – then a reply that starts with **"In order for you to get a promotion, you would need to . . . "** would be a really good way to begin, because this tells them that you are directly answering what they have asked. If, instead, you started by describing the company's policies around promotion and how they happen in general terms, the person may feel that they are just being given the standard company response: being brushed off rather than given an answer that is unique and specific to them.

Again, the more that people feel their questions are being answered directly, the greater the rapport that is built and the commitment to the conversation on both sides. If we don't feel our questions are being answered directly, or we believe that people are giving us a brush-off, we are very likely to disengage from the conversation and not take seriously anything else the other person says to us.

One important thing to consider, when you are in a group environment and one individual keeps asking you several questions, is "Why do they keep asking questions?" Is it because they don't understand, are they trying to prove you wrong or are they just showing off how much they know on the subject in front of other people? This sort of thing can happen in a training environment, but also happens in a social environment as well.

In a business or training environment where someone is asking a lot of questions, one way to spot if they are merely trying to show off how much they know is through the words they use. Very typically, a show-off will start their sentence with words like "And isn't it the case that . . . ?"

You can tell from their tonality as well, when they say that statement, that they are sure it is the case and they only want you or the other people in the room to realize just how much they know.

If you get caught in a situation where someone is continually asking question after question, then you may not be helping with the way you are replying to each question. Very often, when people ask us a question in a group situation, we are tempted to look only at that person while answering. This then encourages the person to ask another question, because it feels to them like the two of you are in a one-to-one conversation, and the rest of the people in the group can feel excluded by this. To avoid this, when you are asked a question, start answering while looking at the person who asked it but then make sure you spread your eye contact around the whole group, answering the question to the whole group. This makes everyone feel included and gives far less opportunity for the person who originally asked the question to come back with another question and engage you in a one-to-one conversation.

How Much Detail?

Another important consideration in a discussion, or when answering a question, is "How much detail does the person really want?" You can make or break a connection by giving too much detail or not enough. In life, whether we want a lot of detail or we just want to know the big, overall picture of things varies for each of us for different aspects of our life.

A great example of this would be when my wife and I are speaking about getting new furniture for our home, like a new sofa. With regards to the amount of detail that's important to me with respect to a new sofa, I am very big picture. Basically, if it looks okay, fits in the room and you can sit on it, I'm happy. My wife, however, has a much more detailed approach to this subject. She wants to know about the material. She wants to know how durable it is. She wants to know about the stain removal factors involved in the material it is made of, the style and curves and how that may complement or go against the other furniture in the room, the type of cushions that may well go with the sofa. There are many, many different factors and elements involved around the whole subject of getting a new sofa as far as my wife is concerned. She is very detailed, therefore, in this particular context.

However, when the attention turns to getting a new car, my wife is very big picture: as long as it's black, has got cup holders, she can control the stereo from her steering wheel and it has heated seats, she is pretty well sorted. But I want to know about the performance, the fuel consumption, the engine size, the type of fuel system; I want to know about the wheel size and the profile of the tyres. Yes, I am very, very detailed in this aspect or context of life.

So, as you can see, we can't make assumptions about people and say, "That person is very big picture or very summary level and this person over here is very detailed". We all will exhibit both detail and big picture views of things for different contexts or areas of life.

If you are in a situation where someone is really just looking for the big picture, but you give them lots of detail, they are likely to become bored and switch off. On the other hand, if you are giving someone who really wants a lot of detail just a very high level or big picture answer, then they are likely to have too many unanswered questions going on in their head in order to buy in or agree with what you are saying.

One way around this is to simply ask them **"How much detail would you like?"** Or, if you've just given a big overview summary ask, **"What else would you like to know about in detail?"**; **"Is there anything else I can tell you about this?"** In most cases, it's safer to start with the big overview and then ask where they would like more detail than vice versa. If you start with the detail, you can't really go backwards if the person only wanted a high-level overview, because you've already given all the detail out.

Sometimes though, you may find it useful to find out what the person wants in a given context in advance. So, do they want the big picture or do they want the detail?

Let's say you want to offer someone an opportunity to get involved in a project and you don't know whether they want to know all the ins and outs, or whether they just want a high-level overview of what you are proposing. You could ask them, **"What was the last project like that you were involved in?"** If they just give you very few facts, that suggests they've got a big picture approach to that particular area of life. If, however, they start telling you every single little detail about the project they were involved in and what they had to do, that might suggest they are very detailed in this area, in which case you could give them more detail as well. It could also be a good idea, in this instance, to ask them what they particularly enjoyed about that project, as this will give you their decision-making strategy or show you what's important to them about such projects. This will then allow you to highlight in the information you pass back to them elements that match what it is they liked or enjoyed about the previous project.

Another example might be if you are looking to hire someone for a particular job and a candidate wants more information about the job. You need to find out straight away whether they want the big picture overview or the nuts and bolts of what the job would involve. You could simply just ask them **"So what was your last job then and what were your roles and responsibilities?"** If they just say on a high level "I was the area sales manager responsible for the whole of the eastern region", they have given a big picture type answer. If, however, they start by saying, "Well, I was the area sales manager responsible for the eastern region. I had to get all of the team together on a weekly basis. We'd meet at 10:00 am on a Monday morning. We'd plan our strategy for the week and then in the afternoon what we would do is this . . . " Already you can see here that we are dealing with a detailed person and they may well be interested in a similar level of detail regarding the opportunity that you have on offer.

Exercise

Perhaps you might like to pause for a moment now and think about in what areas of your life you are very detailed and in what other areas of your life you are very big picture and only want the overview.

The Balance of Consistency and Variety

The area of consistency and variety is also important to consider when you are looking to get someone involved in something. We all look for and need consistency and variety in our lives but where we look for it and how we look for it varies greatly from person to person. A lot of people have in common the fact that they like the consistency of knowing where they live – they perhaps have a house where they live and go to after work each day. It would also probably be true of most people that they like the variety of knowing that when they receive presents at Christmas, for example, every present will probably be different when they open it.

Imagine that these two elements were the other way around. If you didn't know each day after leaving work where you would be sleeping that night, and all the presents you received at Christmas were exactly the same; it's probably safe to assume you wouldn't be very content with those arrangements.

Outside of these two extreme examples, though, we tend to differ from person to person on where we like consistency and where we like variety. Some people like variety with holidays and will go to different places every year and experience different things. Other people like consistency with holidays, choosing to go to the same place because it's familiar, they know what they'll be doing, they know how things work and they look forward to experiencing something very similar and consistent with what they have experienced in previous years.

The same is true of the jobs we do or the careers that we have. Some people will like variety in their job or career. When they go to work every day, they enjoy the fact that they don't know what's going to happen next or what the day ahead will hold for them. These people tend to need to be very reactive, think on their feet, come up with ideas and solutions in a very short period of time and react to whatever is going on during the day pretty much as it happens. Other people, though, look for consistency when it comes to work. They like to know every day when they get in to work what they have to do and when; there are no shocks or surprises. So these two types of people have a very different approach to the sorts of things they like about the job or career that they do.

Someone really looking for consistency would love terms like "step-by-step", "process" or "procedure". People who love variety will typically be attracted by terms like "work on your own initiative", "plan your own day", "you decide what happens when" or "thinking on your feet".

You can find out relatively easily from someone which way they tend to lean for any given topic or aspect of life. For instance, with a holiday you could say, **"What do you like about being on holiday?"** and if they didn't start talking about things being the same or having variety, you could delve deeper by asking them something like **"So, do you like a holiday that's completely different each year or do you like to know in advance what your holiday is going to be like and typically like to do the same things?"**

For some elements of life, it can be quite important to know what way a person leans in a given context or aspect of it. Take jobs and careers, for example. If you are looking for a marketing person, you probably want someone who enjoys variety and coming up with new ideas, who is creative, who doesn't know what's going to happen next and can react to that and come up with strategies and plans to move the business forward no matter what goes on. However, if you are looking to hire someone as a health and safety manager, then you really want somebody who is probably going to be more concerned with following procedures. There are a number of rules, laws and procedures involved in health and safety, including all the checks that need to be done and reports that need to be filled out. So, if you were looking for a health and safety person, you would probably want to make sure that their approach to jobs and careers was one of consistency and procedure.

However, during a conversation, you can engage someone to look at something that may not totally align with the way they normally look at that aspect of life. For instance, if you've got a consistency or procedures-based person and you are talking about them getting involved in something that has a lot of variety to it, you can look at the individual elements involved in the activity and find out what the consistent elements are. You are then able to point these out, despite all the variety in the project. Hopefully that may be enough to give the other person a degree of comfort about getting involved. Likewise, if you've got something that has a lot of consistency but the person you are dealing with likes variety, then you can look at what parts of the activity or project do have variety.

A Little Recognition and Appreciation Goes a Long Way

Recognition and gratitude can be two of the best ways to build rapport and motivate people. All too often in business, not enough gratitude or recognition is given to team members. Even just a casual, passing comment of **"You did a great job on that one"** will build huge appreciation in the team member involved and motivate them to do a good job next time or to go on and look for even more recognition. The lack of recognition out in the business world constantly amazes me, especially between managers and team members, when just saying a few words where they are justified and giving someone that recognition can greatly improve morale and productivity.

Some team members actually need a lot of recognition from their manager, co-workers, customers or clients. Other team members don't really need any recognition. So why are they different? Well, some people are very externally based when it comes to recognition and that means they look outside themselves for recognition in a particular activity. Hence, with regard to doing their job or work, for instance, if they are very external, they will look for somebody else to tell them they have done a good job. However, someone that's very internally focused with regards to recognition on the job they do will typically not look to other people for recognition; they will look inside themselves and simply know whether they did do a good job or not.

You can quite easily find out which way someone looks for recognition, for instance in a job, by simply asking the question **"How do you know when you've done a good job?"** Someone who is internally focused will say something like "Well, I just know I have. I know when I have done a good job." And the interesting thing about the extremely internally focused person is that, even if someone else criticizes and says that they have done a bad job, they will come back with "No, I haven't. I have done a good job and I know I have. You don't know what you are talking about." When asked "How do you know you have done a good job?" a person who is heavily externally referenced with regards to knowing when they have done a good job will typically reply along the lines of "When my manager tells me" or "When my clients and customers tell me".

Now, it is rare to find anyone totally at one extreme or the other with regard to looking internally or externally for recognition. We're all somewhere along the line between the two extremes and it changes from context to context and in different aspects of life as well. The important point to remember, though, is that a little recognition and appreciation goes a long way: so, if you can build recognition and appreciation into your conversations, then you are going to move that relationship on to another level.

Exercise

So, how do you look for recognition in your job or career? Are you internally focused or externally focused most of the time? Think back to the section where we were looking at consistency and variety; how does that stack up for your job or career? Do you look for consistency – knowing what you are going to be doing every day – or do you like variety – not knowing what's going to happen from day to day and thriving on the unknown?

Are You Really Listening?

The person you are talking to wants to know that you are really listening and engaged with what they are telling you. This is why it is important to listen and to ask questions or pass comments that are directly related to what the other person has just explained to you. So many people say – and it is true – that a good way of achieving this is to start your question or next statement with the ending of what the other person just spoke about. For example, if they said something like " . . . and that was a really, really good weekend for me", you would start the next line of your statement with **"That's brilliant that you had a really good weekend there then . . . "** In this way you have acknowledged that you have listened to what they said because you have used part of what they said in the start of your response.

Eye contact is also a very important way of letting people know you are fully engaged with them. While talking to someone it's important to make occasional eye contact, especially when listening to them, and include the occasional smile or facial expression that is relevant to what is being discussed at the time. You really need to avoid looking over that person's shoulder to other things that are going on in the environment and causing a distraction because this could be interpreted as meaning that you are not really listening to them or that you are perhaps getting a bit bored with the conversation.

It is natural if anyone moves around in our peripheral eye space, of course, for us to glance away slightly. It is part of an inbuilt human defence mechanism, so don't be put off if you do this very occasionally. But consciously avoid making a habit of it, especially when you are looking at someone else and perhaps thinking, "Oh, I need to talk to that person later". It can become very obvious to the person you are currently in a conversation with that you have disengaged, because you typically glance away and disconnect for longer than the casual glance to see who has just moved into your peripheral space.

Of course another way to reassure people that you are listening is to nod at different points when they state different interesting facts – just acknowledge with body language and facial expressions that you are listening to what they are saying and that you are interested in it.

I have met a number of people who have felt that other people don't really want to engage in conversation with them. They often feel they are being given the brush-off by others. What I have found in most of these situations is that the person isn't actually managing the connection and the conversation in the right way. As a consequence, this forces the other person to disengage. Now, this hasn't always been intentional on their part. In one particular case, I noticed something quite unique with someone I was mentoring. They had told me that whenever they go to networking events, no one wants to talk to them and they think that the problem is that they must talk about things that other people find boring. They came to this conclusion because after a while of talking to someone that person often starts looking over their shoulder and looking for other people to talk to, becoming completely disconnected from the conversation.

I discovered, while they were talking to me, that I too was getting disconnected from their conversation and saw for myself, by observation, what was going on. Most people, when having a conversation with someone, need to pause and think about something or consider something before responding. We typically either slow our speed of speech down or look away slightly and look up whilst we are thinking and then turn back to the person and respond. What happens is, whilst we may have broken eye contact, the person knows because of the pause in our conversation and the slowing down of our speech that we are thinking about our answer. So, we are still really engaged in the conversation. However, when this person was talking to me, when they looked away or up to think about their next answer, they kept talking. They kept filling in the gaps at the same pace they normally spoke at.

This made it seem to me, and others no doubt, that they were not interested in the conversation. They were breaking rapport because they were actually talking to me but looking in the complete other direction across the room, which made me feel uneasy. I didn't feel like I could take onboard everything they were saying while they weren't looking at me and yet still talking normally. I then, of course, brought this to their attention and suggested that they needed to practise this: in a conversation, when they need to think about something, they should slow down their talking speed and pause while thinking about their next statement so that the other person really does know that they have looked away just because they are thinking of a response – not because they are not interested in the conversation.

I don't believe it was the case that the people they were talking to were thinking, "They're not interested in the conversation because they're looking away". I think this was all happening on a subconscious level where they didn't feel the connection. Looking away and carrying on the conversation without any eye contact caused the connection to break. It's almost like that "they'd rather not be here" type of feeling. Be conscious of this and show signs to acknowledge to the other person that you are listening.

What's in a name?

In *How To Win Friends and Influence People* by Dale Carnegie, it was said that a person's name is the sweetest sound they will ever hear. This is just as true today as it was when that was first written many years ago. You can take the connection to the next level simply by using the other person's name a couple of times in a conversation. The important thing here is not to overdo it. If you are constantly saying their name every other sentence, then it has the complete opposite effect and rapidly reduces the connection.

I myself have experienced this on a number of occasions with someone who was trying to be over-the-top sales orientated. I was dealing with a sales person who pretty much used my name in every single sentence they were saying – things like "It's really good to see you, Mark. I am sure we're going to be able to put a lot of things together for you, Mark. And what you're going to find Mark, is at the end of this you're going to really walk away Mark, knowing that you have made a great decision" – just far too many uses of my name in there. If they'd just used my name once or twice, that would have been great and it would have felt like we were closer or friendlier towards each other. However, constantly saying my name time and time again had the opposite effect.

Of course, sometimes in a conversation we can be talking to someone, especially in a public scenario, and not even know what their name is. However, if we get to a point where we have been talking for some time, it is relatively easy to bring up the subject of exchanging names simply by saying, **"Sorry. My name is Mark, by the way."** They will then respond with their name and the name exchange has taken place.

People often have a problem remembering names when they are talking to new people and being introduced. This usually comes down to the fact that they were not really paying attention and listening when the other person said what their name was. Instead they were listening to their own inner voice figuring out what they were going to say next in the conversation.

A little trick I use myself to help remember names is as soon as someone tells me their name, I try and think of someone that I know with the same first name. And if I can think of someone I know with the same first name then, in my mind, I picture them alongside the person in front of me. If I don't know anyone with the same name then I will see if I can make up a quick rhyme in my head that I will remember them by. For example, if they said their name was Bob and I didn't have anyone I could associate that name with,

I might make up the rhyme in my head saying, "Bob's got a good job", for instance. Another technique people use for remembering names is repeating the name in their head three or four times to themselves when the other person says what their name is, or they simply say out loud **"Well, it's great to meet you . . . "** followed by the name they've just been told. Again, this is another way of getting better at remembering names.

In some conversations you are not looking for anything beyond making a connection and being understood. However, if you need the other person to agree with you on something or do something, then Stage 4 will show you how to lead them to taking action.

10
Stage 4 – Get Them to Take Action

You have started talking to someone. You have generated curiosity and interest. They feel like you understand them and a real connection has been made. So, now we'll look at how to get them to take action. Perhaps this might be closing a sale in a business transaction or securing someone's agreement to go on a trip or undertake an activity with you, or simply to agree with you about what you may be doing together later that day.

This is all about doing it in a way that isn't confrontational and doesn't make anyone feel awkward. It's almost as if they end up going the way you'd like them to go due to all the previous steps you've made in your conversation so far – from the last few stages and this one. More often than not it seems like the natural thing for them to do.

In order for someone to do something or decide to do something, they need to feel enthusiastic about it; and in order for them to be enthusiastic about it you need to be enthusiastic about it as well. So, your enthusiasm needs to come across naturally. You find the enthusiasm in what it is you are looking to do together. You imagine yourselves doing whatever it is together and then you let that enthusiasm come out in your communication. It will come out naturally through your tonality, your body language and the words that you use.

People are attracted to and want to be part of genuine enthusiasm. It is miles away from desperation and being pushy. We sense desperation and pushiness and we pull back from them. We also, on a subconscious level, sense enthusiasm and are generally swept along with it.

At a general high level, getting someone to take action or make a decision could be summarized in two simple steps. Firstly, ask them and, secondly, follow up until it happens. Also, let them know that you will follow up if the decision or action is not going to be immediate. This will create a sense of accountability and make it more likely that they will take that action or make that decision.

Whilst this won't apply to every aspect of life and communication, it is a good guide to remember something that was said some time ago. The way to make somebody want something is to make sure you demonstrate the value in what is being offered. Then show them that other people like it as well. This gives it credibility. If other people like it – other people are doing it or engaged in it – the assumption is it must be good, especially if those people that you are demonstrating like it are people that other people either know or respect or may have heard of.

The next step is to give it some scarcity, either with a limited availability or a limited time in which to make the decision. It can also be useful to make people earn it. Don't make it too easy for them to get it. We tend to want things that we think there is a chance we might not get. So we could achieve this last step by saying something like **"But I'm not completely sure this would be right for you"**. This gives them an opportunity to prove themselves. People love to qualify, be approved or get validated.

Of course we also need to remember, from the previous chapters, to focus on what's important to the other person, something we should have already found out earlier in our conversation. We should be using what's important to them in this stage of attempting to get them to take action, reminding them that this does include what's important to them.

Let's now look at some of the other elements that go into the decision-making process in a bit more detail.

Motivation

In order to take action in life, we need to be motivated. We need a degree of motivation in order to do anything. You have heard of the carrot and the stick. You will probably find that in some aspects of your life you are motivated by the stick, i.e. you do something because of the downside or the consequences of not doing it. At other times you are motivated by the carrot, whereby you are taking action because of the excitement or the good outcome that you will get from doing it. This is also often referred to as moving away from pain or moving towards pleasure. Both work, although there are some interesting differences to each approach.

For example, imagine a situation where there are two people both struggling financially to pay their bills. They both need to take action and they know things need to change. One of them motivates themselves by thinking about all of the good things the future would hold for them if they took some action and changed things in their lives – thinking about how great it would be to not worry about the bills anymore and to have money to do the things that they'd like to do in their lives. This person is using a "motivated-towards" strategy, or the carrot.

The other person may motivate themselves to action by thinking about all the bad things that could happen if they don't make a change. This is a "motivated-away" strategy, or the stick. They might start thinking about running out of money, not being able to put food on the table, the bailiffs coming round, perhaps even the shame of friends and family realizing the bad situation they're in.

Now, both of these strategies can work, although sometimes with different consequences. For instance, in this example the person motivated by the good outcome is more likely to be enthusiastic and a happier person to be around. On the other hand, the person motivated by the stick or the bad outcome may not be the happiest person to be around, because they are constantly thinking about all the bad things that could be happening.

In this particular example of personal finances there is another interesting aspect of the carrot or stick motivation. You may have come across people who get out of a bad situation, start to make headway, get ahead, perhaps financially their lives improve greatly and then they drop back down again. And then they improve again. And then they drop back down again. This can often be an indication of a moving-away-from strategy or the use of the stick.

So why is this? Well, because the person is motivating themselves to action by thinking about all the bad things that could happen if they don't improve things. Then, whilst they do take action and get moving on things, they take their foot off the pedal as soon as they get far enough away from the originally imagined danger and things drop back again. They then approach the point of danger again and take action and, once more, as soon as they are away from the danger, or what they perceive as far enough away, they stop taking the actions they're taking and drop back again.

The person motivated towards the great outcome takes action as well but is more likely to continue doing this, because they start to see the positive effects of the good outcome and are motivated to stick with it. Very often, even if they do drop off a bit, they're likely to reengage quickly to strive for the good outcome again.

So, in your quest to get someone to take action or make a decision, it can be useful for you to know whether in this scenario they are motivated by the carrot or stick. There are clues in what they say because language reflects our inner thinking experiences.

Words and phrases like "getting rid of something" or "overcoming something" or "being free of something" all indicate a moving-away-from strategy – getting away from a bad outcome. Language such as "achieving", "getting", "gaining" or "obtaining" on the other hand is an indication of a moving-towards strategy or the carrot.

When you know which strategy someone is using, then you can use the appropriate words and examples associated with that strategy or way of thinking in order to motivate them to take action. Now, just because you discover that someone may use a motivated-towards strategy in what you are talking to them about in this situation doesn't mean they apply that strategy in all aspects of their life. You will find that most people use a mix of away-from and towards strategies in different aspects of their lives.

For instance, if I need to make a sales call to a potential client, I will motivate myself towards doing that by thinking about how great it will be if they become a client. However, sometimes I have to write reports and appraisals, which I don't enjoy doing very much. I will often motivate myself to do these reports by wanting to avoid being in the situation where I let the client down and don't get the report done on time. Sometimes I'll even use a mix of the two. I'll be thinking about avoiding letting the client down but also be thinking about how good I will feel once it's finished. So I am "moving towards" the good feeling of it being done and out of the way and "away from" letting the client down. So I'm actually mixing both strategies for that particular aspect or context of my life.

Exercise

When you think about yourself and your goals for the future or what you'd like to be in the future, do you think about getting away from where you currently are or do you think about going towards where you want to be? It may even be a mix of the two. Which one do you think feels more powerful or more motivating to you? Do you feel more like you want to go for it to get away from the downside or towards the upside?

Talk as if It's Going to Happen

To get people to take action or make a decision, you need to build their desire to go for it and capture their imagination. This can be done by getting them to imagine themselves in the situation (and feeling good about it) that you want to drive them towards. Talk as if they are already doing it or talk as if they are going to do it. So, rather than say things like "If you were to become a client", you would say things like **"As a client of ours, we will be doing this together"**, **"What we will start doing next month when we are working together is . . . "** or **"Imagine the situation where you are working with us, we're involved in a project and we are doing . . . "** You should also use any of their "key criteria" words that are important to them. As explored in Chapter 9, using these when you are explaining the opportunity or moving towards a decision can really help.

So you're talking as if it's going to happen. You are assuming it's going to happen. You are presuming they are going to be part of it and your words and language assume it is going to happen. Every time in a conversation that you say, "If you were to" – or something along those lines – you are mentally asking that person to re-evaluate their decision whether they are going to or not. Now, this might be too soon, in that you don't want them making the decision at that point because you have got more great information to share with them in order to motivate them to the decision you want them to take.

Capture Their Imagination

A great example of the opportunity to capture someone's imagination is in an interview-type situation. Let's say you are being interviewed for a job and they are telling you about the role and the responsibilities and asking you about your previous experience and so on. Now a real key phrase to use or question to ask could be along the lines of **"Could I just ask you what my first day would be like working in this role?"** Now, in order to answer this question, the interviewer has to imagine you working in the role. So perhaps on the first day you'd be introduced to other team members, you'd have to get together with the personnel department, you'd have to undertake some training and so on. They are going to explain this to you and, when they are explaining this to you, they are going to imagine taking you around the building on the first day to all of these different departments and going through all those parts of the process.

So what does this mean? Well, later on when they are reviewing all the CVs of the applicants and their interview notes, when they get to yours they are going to have already imagined you in the job, so there is a chance that they are going to feel it's more natural for you to be in the role than someone else. Now, of course this doesn't guarantee you are going to get the job. There are many other factors involved. But it's another small building block towards making that person feel comfortable about a decision. They've already imagined you in the job so it doesn't seem totally unreal that you would actually be in the job.

Have the Expectation of a Good Outcome

I have mentioned this previously, but it is so important it warrants its own section here. If you have the expectation of a good outcome, you will have a much higher chance of achieving a successful outcome to your communication or the decision you want the other person to take. When you expect a good outcome, it changes your body language, your tonality and the words that you use. This, in turn, affects the way the other person processes what you say and they are far more likely to engage and follow your lead when you have an expectation of a good outcome yourself. Many times before I have seen the situation where someone expects a good outcome and it happens. Likewise, when someone expects a bad outcome, this is exactly what they get. When working with business owners, I am constantly amazed to find out how many go to a sales meeting without the expectation of getting the deal, or who go for an appraisal without the expectation of getting the promotion they want.

Two people can say the exact same thing to a third person on separate occasions and both get a very different response, purely based on how they came across. How they came across was based partly on whether they expected a good outcome or a bad outcome from that interaction. When we are expecting a bad outcome, then the other person that we are engaged with doesn't feel right about the conversation or doesn't feel right about the situation in general.

Go For It!

So you have considered their motivation strategies, you have captured their imagination, you have got an expectation of a good outcome – how do you move on to what we would call "getting the decision" or the "close point" where you are aiming for the other person to go for it and take action? A good way to approach this is not to intend to force people into a corner and put them on the spot. I like to do what I call a "test close" where I float the idea of moving forwards to them and see what their responses are. In order to do this, I may simply say, **"So what's your current thinking?"** and wait for their response. This gives them an opportunity to raise any other questions or concerns they have or for me to see if they are unsure about something. I can then attempt to address any concerns or questions they have and hopefully bring us to a point where we can move forward.

Another good way of working towards closing out a situation is to find out how the other person would like to move things forward. You can achieve this by asking something like, **"What would have to happen in order for us to proceed with this?"**, **"What would we need to do in order to make this work?"** or **"What steps should we take in order to move this forward?"** Again, this will bring up any questions or concerns or let you know what will make them feel comfortable about moving things forward.

Sometimes people say, "Yes", which is great. Other times, they say, "No". However, a common response to a lot of situations is "I just need to think about it".

When someone says this to you, what would you generally do? Most people say, "Okay then, let me know". In this situation they have given up control of the conversation and of the decision process. I find a really great way to deal with "I need to think about it" is to simply reply, **"That's great. Of course you do. But could I just ask what specifically do you need to think about?"** When you know what it is they need to think about, you may be able to help them resolve some of those things or at least know what to check up on when you follow up with them in a few days or the following week. You want to come away from the "I just need to think about it" situation with a list of things they want to think about. Then, when you follow up with them, you simply are asking, **"So what happened about each of those things?"** As far as you are concerned, once those items have been crossed off the list and resolved, they are then ready to move forward.

Often people are hesitant to follow up in the future and find it awkward if they don't get a yes or agreement straight away. A great way around this is to make your follow-up expected. Once you've collected all of the information that they need to think about, before you leave them and go your separate ways you could simply say, **"Well thanks for your time. I will give you a call next week to see how things are going."**

Then when you call the next week, you remind them that you said you would call. So you might open the conversation with something like **"Hi there. I am just giving you a call this week like I said I would last week when we met to find out how you got on with . . . "** and then mention one of the things that they needed to think about. Once they've been through everything and have addressed all the issues, you can go back to where you started and simply ask the original question again – **"So what's your current thinking?"** or **"Given that you've got all of the unresolved items resolved now, what now needs to happen in order for us to move this forward?"**

Narrow Choices Are Best!

In effective communication it is better to force people to make a choice rather than ask them if they want to do something. So, rather than say, "Shall we get together next week and talk further about this?" you would be far better saying, **"What day would you like to get together next week to talk about this, Tuesday or Wednesday?"** This creates an expectation, rather than the mere suggestion, that you are going to get together next week. There is a much higher chance that you will be getting together next week for a meeting if you give a narrow choice like this. This is also used a lot in sales and called a "double bind". So, rather than saying, "Would you like to buy one of these?" the sales person would be saying, "Which one would you like to buy – Product A or Product B?" hence implying the prospect is going to buy one of them.

Of course, it doesn't guarantee a result every time but it does guarantee that on more occasions people will be going along with you rather than resisting what it is that you are proposing at that point in time. You see, in pretty much any situation in life there are those people that will always say "yes" and there are also those people that will always say "no". What we are looking at though – with our communication – is moving the undecided people, the people that might do something, from a "might do something" to a "yes". We can also convert a lot of "no's" to "yes" as well, of course.

Objections

Sometimes when people are not going to move forwards, they will give an objection or a reason for it. It's important for you to understand that the objection people give you isn't always the real reason why they are not moving forwards.

People seem to have a stock reason that they use to get out of situations such as "I haven't got any time" or "Due to the economy at the moment, we're not looking to do anything". One way you can attempt to move past this is to simply respond with something like **"Well thank you for telling me this, but could I just ask if that were not to be a problem, would you then be moving forwards?"** Sometimes they say "Yes" and sometimes they say "No". What I have found is that in many cases, the real reason is a different one and once you say the line **"If that wasn't a problem, would you then be moving forwards?"** then you very often find out what the real reason is for not moving forward and perhaps have an opportunity to change that.

Conclusion

In order to take any action people need to be enthusiastic about and/or motivated towards the action. Usually people are far more likely to be enthusiastic about something if you are as well. It can be quite tricky trying to get someone else enthusiastic about something you have no enthusiasm for yourself!

Understanding the way the other person is motivating themselves in a given situation (carrot or stick) helps you align their motivation strategy with the decision you are hoping they will make. Are they looking to move towards some great outcome or escape the bad outcome?

Your confidence that they will make the decision you want them to makes it much more likely that they will. *When* you start talking about what it will be like when you are doing something together, rather than *if* you do something together, they engage in the experience differently. This means they imagine it happening and, therefore, there is more chance it will.

Summary of the Stages of an Interaction

This chapter brings us to the end of the four stages of an interaction. They were:

Stage 1 – Your outcome and starting a conversation.
Stage 2 – Creating curiosity and interest.
Stage 3 – Making a connection and being understood.
Stage 4 – Getting people to take action.

If you have opened well (Stage 1) and gone on to create curiosity and interest (Stage 2), then really made a connection with someone such that they feel understood (Stage 3), then action (Stage 4) usually follows naturally. If the action doesn't follow naturally, you simply ask.

Of course there will be times part way through the stages when you decide that whatever you are looking to do isn't right for the other person, in which case the conversation ends before getting to Stage 4.

A lot of the time when people tell me their Stage 4 isn't working, I discover that the situation is obviously not right for the other person involved. Remember this is all about helping people think through and see the real benefits to them. It is not about persuading people towards something of no benefit to them.

Now you have the four main stages taken care of it's time to polish up your communication skills a little more in Part Three, where you'll be equipped with ideas to get even better results from your conversations.

We will look at how you can make your communication even better through effective use of your voice plus we'll explore handling some difficult conversations and situations. We'll also look at the common pitfalls to avoid when talking to people.

PART THREE

Making Your Communication Even Better

11
Making Your Voice Work for You

This chapter looks at some additional language techniques and how you can use them, based on your tonality and other aspects of your voice, to influence the way somebody takes on board the information you are telling them. These techniques will help you enhance the skills you've learnt in the four main stages and get even better results from your conversations. They will help your conversations to be more interesting and engaging and contribute to far greater rapport and connection.

Tonality

The meaning of any communication is more about the tonality and tone of voice used than the actual words themselves. Therefore, it is important to take care with the tonality you are using. For instance, the same words can be said in a certain tonality such that they are taken as being a joke or humorous and another way such that they are taken very seriously. A great example would be the phrase "Get out of here". That could be said in a stern, telling-off tonality or it could be said in an amazed and unbelievable tonality. Both situations use the exact same words but the meaning is completely different based on the tonality used.

Tonality is also important in keeping people interested in what you are saying. So, when you are talking to people about an experience or something that has gone on, it is important to be aware of the tonality that you are using.

Use tonality to make the words you say have more impact. For instance, you would usually say the word "slowly" in a slow speed of voice so that it sounded like the word itself. And if you were describing something that was "going faster and faster", you would say the words "faster and faster" very quickly. This gives much more meaning and interest to whatever it is you are talking about. Bringing your communication alive by varying your tonality – sounding surprised when you talk about something that surprised you, excited when you are talking about something that excited you and nervous when you are talking about something that made you nervous – will help towards increasing the engagement of the person you are talking to. A varying tonality is far more interesting to listen to than a constant, monotone level where all of your words sound exactly the same.

If you want the other person to be excited about your conversation, you've got to be excited about it yourself first.

Speed of Talking

Another way of building rapport with someone when you are talking to them is to match the speed of their speech.

Therefore, if they are talking quite quickly, you could attempt to talk at a similar pace, providing it isn't too uncomfortably quick for you. Likewise, if the other person is talking quite slowly then you should aim to slow down the speed of your own voice so that you are talking more closely to the speed they are speaking at. Again, we don't want to speak too slowly, such that it's uncomfortable for us, but as best we can match the speed of the other person's voice and words to increase the rapport between us.

It's not just about the rapport when matching the speed of talking either. People tend to understand and process information at different speeds. The speed with which somebody is understanding or processing any situation is often reflected in the speed of their speech. Therefore, if somebody is talking relatively slowly or at a much slower pace than you are, it could be because they are having to think carefully about things. So, if you are speaking too quickly for the other person, they are likely to have trouble understanding you because they cannot process the words at the speed you are saying them.

It happens the other way around as well. If you are talking very slowly compared to the other person, they are likely to be processing information very fast in this instance and could get bored waiting for you to finish each sentence. This is another reason why it is quite important to match the speed of talking with the other person as best you can.

Pauses

It is also important to consider the role of the pause or gap between words in any conversation. A pause can be used for very dramatic effect, to highlight a statement before you continue on to another one, for instance. When an extended pause is given with a certain facial expression, such as the raising of the eyebrows, this can lead the other person to be compelled to answer or contribute to the conversation. It is also important to be fairly animated in conversation, so use your facial expressions and your hands when you are describing different aspects of an experience to the other person.

However, when using your hands to describe things or map out a scene, for example, make sure you keep your hands at waist to chest level. Very often, waving hands higher – above chest level – can start to impede personal space or even be too distracting for people. Funnily enough, one of the reasons that waving your arms too high can be distracting isn't just the fact that the other person thinks they may get hit in the face at any moment. It is also because you are probably waving your hands within the personal space sphere they are using to think – because we think in pictures and we tend to place those pictures out in front of us, relatively.

Intonation

When it comes to looking at the intonation in your voice, this will depend greatly on the culture and traditions of the language that you are using to speak to people with. Even within the English language the use of intonation varies: for example, quite greatly between people in the UK and people in Australia. For now, let's look at the example of two people within the UK who are using the UK English language and engaged in a conversation. Typically, in this situation when we are making a statement our level of voice, volume-wise and pitch-wise, will remain constant. However, if we are asking a question, then typically the pitch in our voice and the volume will tend to rise towards the end of the phrase, i.e. the end of the question. Likewise, if we are giving a command to someone, our intonation – our volume and pitch – will tend to lower at the end of the statement and go downwards. Think about this, for example, in your life. Imagine you are giving somebody a command, i.e. "Do that now"; or you are asking someone a question, such as "How do you do that?"; or you are just making a statement like, "It's sunny today". Can you notice that your intonation, level of voice or pitch changes somewhat between the examples?

When talking with people your voice is your main tool, like the racing car is the main tool of the Grand Prix champion. The car never makes the driver as good as he can be unless it is well tuned. The same is true of the voice techniques in this chapter. They can very often be the difference between you coming in first and getting the result you're after, or running a close second.

12
Common Pitfalls

In this chapter we will take a look at some of the common pitfalls to avoid. These usually occur when something goes wrong (or rather when you believe it has gone wrong) in an interaction.

I Got a Bad Response and Didn't Know How to Handle the Situation

In most situations, if you get a critical comment or response from someone the best way to handle it is as follows.

Just calmly say either:

"That's interesting."

Or

"OK."

In most instances, where someone is critical or gives a bad response, they are expecting one of two outcomes. Either you are going to argue back or you are going to retreat and go away having been humiliated or put in your place.

Said with the right calm, casual tone, the "**That's interesting**" or "**OK**" response confuses them. It is unlikely to escalate a negative situation and it means you do not go away having been put in your place!

Other times, people may use their physical size or presence to make you feel awkward. In this case saying a friendly "**Wow, I should hire you as my bodyguard**" is a non-confrontational comment to respond to the situation. However, there is also a secondary communication element going on here – you've basically implied that you would hire them and that they would work for you!

As you can see with this simple technique, or way of responding, you can now easily deal with those awkward situations if they should ever occur. It is also a response that protects your pride but doesn't escalate the situation further.

We look at dealing with critical comments in more detail in Chapter 13.

Avoid Explaining too Much

Along the same lines of finding out what's important to someone and the level of detail they'd prefer, there is also the aspect of not explaining too much upfront. What I mean by this is, especially in a business situation, if you are looking to present an idea to somebody or they have enquired about something, it can be useful to ask them (as well as what's important to them) if they have got any burning questions upfront. This way, you can find out if there are any aspects of the topic you were about to discuss with them that they are particularly keen to know. Sometimes, if someone has got a burning question, they are not really focused on the rest of the information you are giving them because their mind keeps going back to this burning question they've got and, at the extreme, they could even be looking for clues in what you are saying to try and build evidence to answer this burning question they've got in their mind.

Now, of course, not all burning questions can be answered upfront so it may be that when they tell you what it is you simply need to explain that you'll come back to it later on. A classic example would be if someone says, "Well, how much is all this going to cost?" It may be that until you spend some time with them, finding out exactly what they need, you won't know exactly how much it's going to cost. If they've got a burning desire to know the answer though, so they don't waste time engaging with you only to find out it's out of their budget, then it might be just as well to find some way of reassuring them about the budget range at that point in time. They'll then relax more and engage more fully in the rest of what you are explaining. If they are not engaged with what you are explaining, then you stand little chance of getting them onboard to move them in the direction that you'd like them to go as a result of this conversation that you are having with them.

Use "But" with Caution

When somebody says something to you and you reply or interrupt with the word "but", it tends to suggest that you are probably going to disagree with everything that they have just said. The other person then gets defensive and will just look for more and more evidence to support the case that they were building with their initial statement. A far better way to reply to someone who has a difference of opinion to you is to initially seem to agree with them and then move the conversation on.

For example, say I am in a discussion with somebody about purchasing a car in a particular colour and they say, "I think that red is the best colour for this particular car", if in response to that I reply, "But blue is better", they are likely to just say, "No. I think that red is the best colour" and constantly defend their initial position. However, when faced with someone saying, "I think that car is best in red", I would reply with something along the lines of **"Yes, I can see why you would say that, red is a really, really good colour for the car. Have you noticed the different greens and blues that are available today as well? Because one of the things that the blue and green models bring about is an air of exclusivity because there are very few of them on the road."**

Very often you can substitute where you would normally say the word "but" and use the word "and" instead. When you say the word "and", this suggests to the other person that you agree with them and you are now going to add more detail or information to what they have said. And, in many cases, you could – after you have said the word "and" – completely disagree with them. So, in this car example again, the other person has said to you "I think red is the best colour". You could reply, **"And green is not bad either. In fact, I think the best colour of all is blue. That's because it's a new one they've just brought out and there are very, very few of those models on the road in blue."** What you've done there is appear to agree with them and then moved them on to focusing on your idea of a different colour without appearing to totally disagree with them. It's been a much smoother transition in the discussion.

Respond, Rather Than React

Successful communication, and the outcome, is based upon responding to the other person rather than reacting (or over-reacting). A response is a considered, logical reply that has been thought out after due consideration to what the other person has said. A reaction to something that somebody has said is very typically an emotional response rather than a reply stemming from full consideration of all possibilities. An example of this would be when you come back in to work and somebody says, "A customer has been on the phone complaining". Do you respond or react in this situation? If you react, you are very likely to start saying things like, "Well, we haven't done anything wrong. They must have ordered the wrong thing", whereas if you respond, you are more likely to take a step back, stay calm and say, "**Well, what's been going on? Let's find out the facts and then let's make a decision about what, if anything, we need to do.**" Can you see how responding and reacting are very different?

When we respond rather than react, we typically get the best outcomes. One thing we usually do is consider the other person's point of view as well.

This doesn't mean we are all going to naturally agree, but it does mean that we are going to get a far better outcome and less emotional aggravation than if we constantly steam in with emotional reactions. So it's important to always ask yourself "**Am I responding or reacting here?**"

Exercise

A powerful question when looking at any situation in life is: "**Given what I know about the situation and what the other person has been through, how would I feel in this moment and what sort of things would I be thinking if I were in this situation?**" This helps us take a greater perspective of the other person's point of view and then enables us to respond rather than react. When we respond in this way, having considered to the best of our abilities the other person's point of view, there is far less chance of us getting a negative reaction back from them. They will know and start to understand that we have considered their position and looked at things from all the different possible angles.

Having explored the common pitfalls of a conversation, in Chapter 13 we will take a look at some of the difficult conversations we need to have from time to time. These examples will give you lots of ideas you can adapt and use in your own difficult conversations.

13
Difficult Work and Business Conversations

In the chapters on opening a conversation and building a connection, we focused a lot on everyday social conversations. The reason for this is most conversations with new people start on the general or social side, even if for just a minute or two, before moving onto business. With so much attention given to general/social conversations it is now time to take a look at handling some of the difficult situations in work and business.

In life there are times, at work or in business, when we have to have what some people would term "difficult conversations". This may be doing appraisals for team members; it might be chasing for payments or delegating work to another person. It may even be talking to somebody when they've done something incorrectly. Other examples might be returning something faulty to a shop or having to break bad news to a friend. The best way to demonstrate the approach for dealing with different difficult conversations is to give you a series of real life examples that I have worked with people on.

A Difficult Meeting

One of my clients explained to me that he was not looking forward to attending a client meeting the following week. When I asked him why that was, he went on to explain that as an accountancy firm they have to go in and have an annual review meeting with the client. At this meeting they needed the owner of the business to be in attendance. The owner didn't like attending these meetings and would always prove very difficult indeed. In fact, from the very start of the meeting the owner would say "I really don't have time for this. I've got far better things to do." Then, throughout the meeting, whenever the accountants would ask a question, he would be very difficult in answering them or even avoid answering; always giving the impression that his time was being wasted.

I suspected that whilst, yes, this business owner was probably very busy and did have better things to do, there was also an element of ego at play here. I suggested that my client try something different at the next client meeting. I told him that as soon as he met the owner, he should say in a friendly jokey manner **"Thank you so much for seeing us today. I know you've got far better things to do than to sit in a room with us accountants for an hour asking you endless questions."** My client felt that this was an okay thing to do and could see himself doing it.

When we met up the following month I asked how the meeting had gone. He said it went brilliantly. The client was really friendly and answered all of their questions. Why was that? Well, in this case, from the outset my client apologized for taking up the owner's time and let him know that everyone realized how "important he was" and appreciated that he had far better things to do than sit around answering their questions. It really ticked a number of boxes in the owner's head and meant that he then relaxed and engaged in the meeting. Previously the owner got frustrated and wanted to make sure everyone else in the room knew that he didn't need to waste time in this meeting. The only way that he could get that message across was to constantly create obstacles and be evasive to the questions.

However, because my client has gone in and said, in a manner of speaking, "Yes you are important. Yes you are busy and yes, we are going to ask you a load of stupid questions and waste your time", the owner of the business felt "Okay, they get it". He then relaxed, his ego stroked enough such that he then just engaged in the meeting.

Broken Promises, Missed Deadlines and Similar Situations

By using your communication and words carefully you can deal with these difficult situations easily and stand more chance of getting things remedied, all without upsetting your relationship with the other person.

An example of this in action is a time when I had to chase a client for late payment. The client had agreed that they would pay my invoices within fourteen days, which was, at the time, my standard payment terms for ongoing client mentoring. This was going against their internal policy of thirty-day payments, but in the negotiations of the contract it was clear that we were going to work on my terms.

However, what subsequently happened is that the first few months' payments were taking thirty-five to forty days to come through. A reaction or overreaction would've been to call my client up and immediately launch into a complaint that he was breaking the rules of our contract and, therefore, I wasn't very happy with him. If I'd taken this approach, how do you think that would've left our relationship? It would've been quite awkward for me going in there the following month knowing that we had had a big falling out over invoice payments and that I had, in many ways, implied he had lied to me in the pre-contract negotiations and now wasn't doing what was agreed. Regardless of whether he was actually at fault for holding up the payments, a tactful approach is best in this type of situation.

So, I decided, of course, to do something different. I contacted the client and said to him, **"I don't know if you are aware of this but your accounting department is running under a bit of confusion and the result is they're letting us both down a bit here. It seems that my invoices are not actually being paid until thirty-five or forty days later; whereas, as you know, we are working on the basis of fourteen days. So, perhaps you could have a word with your people in accounts and make them aware of what they're supposed to be doing for us."** By saying "us" and making the accounts department the third party rather than the client,

I was able to get my message across and make him aware of the situation without it causing any direct conflict between the two of us.

I'd come from the perspective that he and I were on the same side, that we'd got this arrangement and it was only going wrong because other people, in his department, were not doing what they were supposed to be doing and what he and I had agreed. Using this approach I managed to preserve the working relationship with the person that engaged me in the contract and still chase up my late payments.

The same logic, principles and approach can be used for many other life situations where deadlines have been missed or agreements broken.

The Price Has Gone Up

A client was in a situation where a member of their team who was very popular with her clients had now been promoted to manager level. This had resulted in their charge-out rate going up, and therefore they would be more expensive to their clients. Once they told their clients that that member of staff was no longer going to be part of the team, because they were a manager now, the clients would, in some cases, insist on having the original member of staff working with them. The concern was that when this happened they'd have to approach the subject of increased cost due to that member of staff's charge-out rate now being higher.

In these situations, it is important to avoid saying things like "This is going to cost you more money". It should be referred to in a slightly different way, so that the other person knows and appreciates that it means it's going to cost them more money but, on the other hand, it's not so harsh in the conversation flow as saying to someone "Yes, you can have that member of staff but it's going to cost you more".

So, we decided the approach would be that when a client said "Oh that's great that the member of staff has become a manager but I'd still like them working on my project", we would respond with **"Well that's fantastic. I know she'd really love to still work on your project and help you out but I do need to let you know that her time is now recorded at a higher rate per hour."** This still gets the message across but it's a little less direct than "It's going to cost you more".

I've had clients experience a similar situation when they offer an initial free consultation and the person they're doing this consultation for takes up quite a bit of time. They start to ask more and more questions, which cross the line from free consultation to paid consultation. The difficulty this often then leads to is "How do we say to the person, because we don't want to lose the client or upset them, that this is now going to be chargeable?" Well, it's similar to the example I used with the new manager. If you feel like you've got to the point where all of the free consultation time has been used up, then simply reply with **"Absolutely, of course I can look at that for you. I do just need to make you aware though that moving on to that moves us out of the free consultation period and I will need to record time against the project."** You see, again, this is a more eloquent and easy going way of saying "It's going to cost you".

The Art of Delegating

People tend to have two main issues with delegating; either they don't do it at all or, when they do it, the work doesn't actually get done on time. People who don't delegate is a whole other topic, but it comes down to *why* won't they delegate. Perhaps they don't trust the other person to do the work correctly or they think people will think they are lazy, as in "Why can't they do it themselves?" and so on. So, there are many reasons why people don't delegate. However, what we're really looking at here, in respect of delegation, is the situation where we want to communicate with someone, ask them to do something for us and get them to do it when we need it done.

If you're going to delegate a piece of work to someone who is already reasonably busy, they have in their mind the order they're going to approach things. So, they'll likely have a mental list of the things that they are working on during that day. The problem you have is that when you delegate something to them and you want it to be done within a specific time period, you've got to make sure that the language and words that you use are such that they prioritize this within that list of things they've already got mentally arranged in their head.

So many times I see delegation fail because the language is too vague. I had a classic case with a client of mine who said that team members just never got the work done on time and, therefore, it was much better for him to do it himself. This all came down to the fact that when he delegated the work he would usually say something like "Could you have a look at this for me today, if at all possible?" Now using the words "if at all possible" meant that if the person receiving the work was already very busy, it wasn't going to be a strong enough request in order for them to prioritize it within that mental list of things they were going to do. So it didn't even get on the radar. Now, one of the reasons they probably said "if at all possible" is because they wanted to soften the delegation request. They didn't want the team member to feel like they were being told to do something and harm the relationship between the two of them.

A lot of people, when delegating, want to get the work done but they don't want to fall out and not be friends with the people they are delegating to. Now, just like with the late payments example, this can also be achieved with the right communication, words and tonality. We could even apologize for delegating and still stand a much greater chance of the work being done. For example, saying something like **"I'm really sorry. I know you're busy already but I need you to look at this for me today. If, for any reason, you're not going to be able to get this completed by 4:30 pm today, please let me know by 2:30 pm."** You see, we've come across friendly with this and we've even apologized for delegating to them! However, we have said "we need you to do this", not "*could* you do it" but "we *need* you to do it", and we've also set definite deadlines with "if, for any reason, you're not going to meet that deadline, let me know with enough advanced notice". Communicating this way maintains the relationship but also ensures a much higher chance of the work being done and being done on time. It's all about getting specific with the language and letting people know exactly what it is that you want, and it doesn't have to be done in a dictatorial fashion.

Work Done Badly

How do you approach the situation when somebody has done a piece of work and it isn't up to standard? Before any communication, as I've said before, you need to decide the outcome you want from the conversation. What you say to the person and how you say it is going to have a great bearing on the outcome of that conversation. So do you want them to be so upset or fed up and annoyed that they want to leave and get a new job, or do you simply want them to learn from the mistake and be able to do it better next time? If you want them to learn from the mistake and be able to do it better next time, then you have to approach it from a standpoint of talking about what they "could've" done rather than what they "should've" done.

And this can even be lightened further by talking to them about it along the lines of **"Do you know what we could've done on this project? We could've done this or this and this. What do you think?"** This way of using the word "we" softens it even further and doesn't make it directed purely at the person, even though they will, of course, know it was them that made the mistake. However, it makes it easier to have the conversation and the conversation is received much better. Asking **"What do you think?"** at the end of it gets their commitment on board as well. Simply blasting in with, "Hey you've done this wrong. You should've done this, this, this and this" is very likely to leave the person feeling bad about the situation and not be helpful for productivity going forward; as well as damaging, to some extent, the relationship between the two of you. I have found, in all aspects of life and business, you can get fantastic results and get what you're looking for all without being harsh and abrasive, and you can do it just through using communication in a carefully planned out way.

Tricky Appraisals

What do you do in the situation where you have to do a review or appraisal for a member of staff and they haven't really been performing well in their job? Well, for a start, the review or appraisal point shouldn't be the first time they hear about it. Really, you should be making people aware when they're not doing things properly as they go rather than saving it all up for three months' time or whenever they get their next appraisal. However, it can always be the case that someone has been advised from time to time during a recent period that things were not being done correctly or were taking too long and yet that still persists, so it has to be dealt with at appraisal time.

So what can you do? How can you raise this and manage through the situation? Well, a great approach, I've found, is to take the standpoint of letting them do most of the talking. To start off, I would simply say, **"So how's it going?"** and then keep quiet and let them talk. If they say just one or two words I will say **"So, anything else? Anything else been going on that you'd like to raise or you'd like to talk about or share with me?"**

Now, I've found that by doing this, most times they will come up with the issue and say "Well, I'm struggling to get the work in on time" or "I think people feel I'm not doing the work quickly enough". Sometimes they won't raise it at all though. This is where you should use an alternative approach by moving on to asking something along these lines: **"I appreciate we're all different. If I were doing your role I'd be aware of how the jobs were running late most of the time. So what can we do to help you improve that?"**

This has raised the issue and said "If I was doing your role I'd be concerned about that myself" and then I've gone on to say **"What can we do to help you improve that?"** They may say "Nothing; I just need to sort it out". But even when they say that you ought to come back with **"Okay, that's brilliant. What is your approach to sort it?"** You must listen to what their approach is and add in and contribute what you can to help, before agreeing with them how you'll manage this going forward and measure the success.

I'm a great fan, in all these situations, of giving people the benefit of the doubt initially, regardless of whether they are taking far too long to do a task or they're making far too many mistakes. I would always approach this from a standpoint of, **"What is it that we can do to help you get better at this?"**, or **"Is there anything we're doing as a company or a department that isn't helping you to be able to either get things more accurate or get things done on time?"** Out of these questions can come good ideas or the person may themselves come to the conclusion that they need to improve. Either way they have come up with the solution. You haven't had to force your ideas or opinions on them. Of course, using the teachings in this book you can encourage people to come up with your ideas themselves.

Another common issue with appraisals is a situation where one particular person seems to be upsetting the rest of the team. Perhaps they're a bit bossy or perhaps they are a bit rude to people, or maybe they are always late or just simply not performing well. You're aware that the person that's coming in for their appraisal is someone who is basically upsetting the rest of the team and isn't very popular or very much liked by the rest of the staff members. How do you approach this? Well, in a similar way to the examples just described, start out with **"How's it going?"**, followed by **"anything else?"** until you get that complete list of what they think things are like and how they think they're getting on out of them. If they've not raised the issue of not being popular with the team, then a great question you can ask them is **"If I were to ask the other team members what they thought about you, what do you think they would say?"** It's amazing the amount of times I've used this myself when faced with someone who is being particularly bossy to other team members, and 99% of the time they have come up with where their faults currently lie. For instance, they may say "I guess they might think I am a bit direct at times". It's a fascinating process to take people through and, again, it isn't confrontational. It is a very elegant way of communicating through what could otherwise be a difficult situation.

Resistance

Another issue that comes up from time to time is when we feel there will be some resistance to something we've requested or proposed. Say, for instance, in a sales situation we might feel that, when we say we're going to call someone the following week to see if they're ready to make a decision, that they may not be up for it. They might not want us to call them next week. So if we simply said "Can I give you a call next week to follow up?", they may turn around and say "Well next week will be too soon" or "I really don't know where I'm at with this. I'll get back to you."

One way to overcome this could be to almost overdramatize the event and say something along the lines of **"Would it be totally inconvenient if I were to call you next week?"** or, as I've heard some people say before in typical pushy selling, and I use this just for a communication example here, **"Would you be totally offended if I was to give you a call next week?"** You see, when you say **"Would you be totally offended if I was to give you a call next week?"** of course very few, if any, people are going to say "Yes, I will be totally offended if you give me a call next week". Therefore, they are going to give permission by default for the call because you've given them two alternatives. Those two alternatives being I call you or you tell me that you're going to be totally offended if I call you. So, I'm not saying use this "will you be totally offended" approach at all. I'm just using it as an example to demonstrate that how you position what you are communicating can greatly affect the response that you get.

Dealing with Critical Comments

When someone makes a critical comment about something, it is best not to disagree with them straight away. As soon as you disagree with them, they will try to justify their case. It implies you are saying they are wrong. Therefore, when faced with a critical statement, it is always a good idea to ask for more information if it is not completely obvious to you exactly what they mean.

So, for instance, if somebody said that a friend of yours or one of your team members was lazy, you could reply and ask, **"In what ways do you find them lazy?"** You would then gain more information about exactly what they meant and this would give you more of an opportunity to reply and, where possible, realign their thinking. So, in this example, they may say that they feel your friend is lazy because they can never be bothered to turn up for appointments on time and they always seem to be running late. Now, taking onboard the idea that you don't immediately disagree, you could continue this conversation by saying something along the lines of **"I could see why you would think that and yes, it is true that they do arrive late on certain occasions and one of the reasons this happens is that they have a lot of commitments around their children at school and, very often, the school runs late on letting the children out of school, which causes them to run behind on their appointments. In fact, we do a lot of things together at the weekends and if anything, they are always early."**

You could then go on to say, **"You know, I've been exactly where you are. I used to think that they were lazy myself, to be honest. But once I understood what was going on with the children and the school, I realized that it wasn't so much that they were lazy, but that circumstances, which tended to happen on an ongoing basis, meant that they greatly underestimated how long it would take them to get to appointments on a weekday."** What you have done here is, firstly, agreed with the person. Then you've found out more about what was going on in order for them to say that this friend or team member is lazy. Having found out that information you have addressed the issue and at the same time explained why this happens. Then you've gone on to suggest to them that the person in question isn't lazy. In fact, the biggest issue is that they simply do not allow enough time and they underestimate the amount of delays that they may face.

People make critical comments for a reason. The skill is in finding out what their reason is; asking them why specifically they think like that. Once you know how they are coming to the critical statement you have the opportunity to respond. Very often people are not operating with all the facts; you can discover this, and fill in the gaps, when you ask them for their specific reasons behind their critical comments.

"I'd Rather Not Discuss That"

Sometimes in a conversation, someone will ask you about something that you really don't want to discuss or go into and how you handle this can affect whether the connection between the two of you is broken or at least make the other person feel really, really awkward in that moment.

When someone asks you something that you really don't want to talk about – maybe it's too painful to talk about or it's a sensitive subject – then, rather than stumble over your words and feel awkward about the whole situation, it is far better to do the following:

1. Say to them in a friendly way **"I am sorry. That's a really sensitive subject right now."**
2. Then immediately, without pausing, in an upbeat and positive way say to them **"So what's been going on with you lately?"** or something else that moves the conversation on quickly.

The important thing here is to respond to what they've asked you in a way that makes it clear that you don't want to talk about that right now while maintaining a friendly tonality and not stopping. Carry on immediately and ask them a question about themselves in a really upbeat way or move on to talking about something else you'd like to talk to them about.

If you were to simply say, "I don't want to talk about that right now" or "That's a sensitive subject" and not continue the flow of conversation and stop, you would probably create an awkward gap in the conversation where the other person feels awkward for asking the question in the first place and also now doesn't know what to do in the gap. That can very quickly make rapport fade and fall away. So always avoid that break and pause, and just skip over it so you bypass any awkwardness, making the whole situation better for both parties involved at that point in time.

Of course there are many other difficult situations and conversations that can occur in life where the same principles can be applied, in work, business and social life. In this chapter we have explored some common difficult conversations in order to highlight the principles in dealing with them, which should help you in your approach to other difficult conversations too.

14
Final Thoughts

A final reminder here, from earlier in the book, before we look at your daily plan of how to implement what you have learnt, that can take you from talking to no one to being able to talk to absolutely anyone.

Communication, or talking to other people, is one of the most important skills that you can develop in life. All of us communicate with other people all of the time.

Once you're able to talk to people you do not know and initiate conversations with them your whole life will expand, you will be more comfortable and relaxed in social and business situations, you will have better experiences and you will learn far more about the world and other people.

A mundane daily chore can become an adventure when you meet and engage with someone new who is interesting, even if that adventure only lasts a minute or two.

The great thing about developing your communication skills is that you can practise every day, many times a day, with conversations you are already having! It takes no additional time to practise and develop this life-changing skill!

Confidence

Of course at the end of the day, like most things in life, it comes down to confidence. Most people will say they lack confidence and do nothing about it. They believe that confidence cannot change. The reason for this is we don't take the time to think about what confidence really is, to understand it. Without understanding something in detail we stand little chance of changing it.

I love the definition of confidence that I heard some years ago, I believe it was world famous Motivational Speaker Tony Robbins.

It was this – "Confidence is our degree of certainty about an outcome we will get, or how we will perform in a given situation."

Thinking about it like this makes it so much easier. If you lack confidence to talk to new people or talk to senior people at work then use the above definition. Ask yourself "What specifically do I lack certainty about?" – is it the outcome, or the actual process of what to say?

In these situations it might be about the outcome – how the other person may react or respond. Or it could be about the process; for example, you don't know what to say. It could be both.

Getting specific is the key.

Once you have these answers you know if you need to develop some skills or change the way you think about it – your mindset.

Start Talking . . .

Now that you've learnt the four stages of an interaction and understand how to get the best out of every conversation, it's time to stop reading and start talking.

Remember, things don't always go really well when starting conversations, but they rarely, if ever, go badly. If they don't go as well as you'd have liked then you have a great story to tell others, about the conversation that started but didn't go too well.

Having this new skill, though, to push on regardless and talk to absolutely anyone that you want to, will set you way ahead of most other people in the world today.

Your "Zero to Hero Talk to Anyone" Development Plan

You now have the knowledge and skills to be able to talk to absolutely anyone.

Hopefully, as you've gone through the book, you have started to use what you have learnt. However, whether you have started taking action or not, your next step is to really get started, keep going and develop the new you.

In order to take you through the next month, the most crucial part of developing and embedding the new you, I have developed for you the "Zero to Hero Talk to Anyone" Development Training Plan, which is Part Four of this book.

The Training Plan takes you from the very start through to gaining confidence and skills from the book and using them on a daily basis.

Before you panic, this plan involves very little time at all – almost none! How come? Because it just asks you to observe or do things within what you are already doing during that day! However, you can go at your own pace and only move on to the next training stage when you are totally ready for it.

Let's get started!

PART FOUR

31 Day "Zero To Hero" Talk To Absolutely Anyone Plan

IMPORTANT NOTES

If you are under medical or professional treatment, share this plan with them and ask them if it is OK for you to do this.

If you are under 18, you MUST tell a parent or adult guardian about this training and get their approval or have them help you with it. You MUST NOT use this training without permission from an adult responsible for your welfare.

It's your responsibility to stay safe. You must make your own judgement call on what is a safe situation to speak to people. A public place like a shopping centre or coffee shop is probably OK, but if they suggest going down a dark alley it's probably not safe!

This book, its entire contents and the training plan that follows is for educational and entertainment use only. It is not to be taken as professional advice; you do anything in this course at your own risk, based on your own judgement.

Introduction

This is how you can go from speaking to no one to being able to talk to absolutely anyone.

What I want to do first is to give you a really good overview of the training course.

The training course is designed to be done a step at a time over the next 31 days. It starts out daily for the first week, then moves to every three days. This section is all about explaining to you how it's going to work and giving you a good overview of each stage that we're going to go through.

The first week is totally focused on getting you to overcome the hesitation to talk to people you don't know. In my experience, most people that want to get better at talking to people they don't know need to overcome some hesitation. So, it's best we get that out of the way. We're also going to look at the beliefs that might be holding you back, and work on changing them and helping you to build some motivation so that you can move forward and push past that hesitation.

Once we've got that sorted, we'll be into getting out there and talking to people. That's going to start on Day 7. We're going to start really, really easy, and we're going to build it up gradually.

So on Day 7, what we're going to do is take everyday occurrences for you where maybe you currently don't say anything or you just say a phrase like "Thank you".

For instance, maybe the mailman delivers you a parcel, you take it and say, "Thank you". Maybe you go to pay for your petrol or gas at the filling station, and you just go in there and say, "Pump 7". And they tell you how much. You give your credit card. They give it back. You say, "Thank you" and walk out. Or you go in a shop to buy something or order a coffee, hand over your money, say. "Thank you" and scamper out of there.

What we're going to look to do in this lesson is to get you to just say a few more words, make a comment about the weather or pass some sort of comment about what's going on in your environment.

So that's what that first lesson is going to be about. It's going to be safe. It's going to be people that work in shops, or perhaps work in a courier service. This is a very safe environment to start saying a little bit more than you currently say so that you can see people's reactions to you and start to get a bit more confidence. Remember, this comes after we have dealt with reducing your fear and hesitation.

After Day 7 we move on to Day 10, because we're going to have three days between each lesson to give you time to practise what comes up in each one.

And this stage of the plan is Level 1, talking to strangers in motion. On Day 10, what we're going to do is talk to a random and complete stranger. Now don't panic, because this is going to be easy. This is going to be what I call "the in-motion passing comment".

We're not looking to engage anyone in conversation. We're not looking to talk to someone for any period of time. It's just about a random, one-off throwaway comment, such as perhaps it's a windy day, and you're walking past someone as you've got a ticket for your parking, and there's someone walking towards you going to get their ticket. And you just say something simple like, "Wow, it's windy today, isn't it?" Or you're walking down the street and there's somebody coming along. They're walking with a particular dog that you don't see many of, and you just say, "Wow, you don't see many of those dogs these days", and you just keep walking.

So the idea is that you'll make brief eye contact with the person. You'll make this throwaway comment. You're not looking to engage anyone in conversation. You're doing it while you're walking, and the other person is walking in the opposite direction. So you're both in motion, and you're just going to keep going. It might even be something like, "It's busy in here" or something like that if you're walking into somewhere.

Then, on Day 13, we're going to step things up a little bit.

Remember, in the previous step, what we were making was a passing comment in motion while we were walking. So there was no awkward standstill or quiet moment there. What we will do on Day 13 is very similar, except that it's in a static situation. This is where you're standing still when speaking, so there's no easy option to run away here because you're going to be in that situation before your comment, during your comment, and after your comment.

So, a great example is perhaps waiting in line in a shop or a store, or waiting in line at the bank, and you say something to someone in front of you about the long line that you're in. You might say something like, "You'd have thought they'd put more cashiers on at lunchtime when it's busy in here, wouldn't you?" or "I'd just love to find the time to come here when it's not too busy"; just some very simple passing comment where you and the person you're talking to are stationary. They may just nod, acknowledge you, or whatever. It doesn't matter. In fact, we're not even interested in their response or if they don't give a response, because we're just looking to put this out there. Of course, if they don't give a response, it probably means they didn't hear you or they didn't think you were talking to them.

Maybe you're waiting to cross a busy road, and you say to someone who's also waiting to cross, "You'd think they'd put a crossing here, wouldn't you?" - just something simple like that, that doesn't really demand a response, but it gets you saying something, overcoming the hesitation and putting something out there. Practise this over a few days, and then you'll move on to the next step of the programme; Day 16.

On Day 16, we ramp it up a little bit more, because what we're going to do here is ask for help: simply asking someone the time. When we're out and about, we're going to ask somebody if they've got the time.

Then we're going to do something on Day 19 which has a little bit more vulnerability to it, because we're going to ask for directions. We're going to ask the way to the nearest Starbucks, Costa Coffee, library or something like that. So, we're going to be focused on asking for directions when we get to Day 19.

And remember; the reason you've got the three-day gap is so that you can practise over the three days. You've got three days to get this sorted and to practise when the opportunity comes up. Now, you can't say "Well, I didn't have time to do it". This is part of your everyday life, whether you're on the way to college, work, whatever, building it into that process. I'm sure you're going to shops or stores. You're seeing people as a natural part of your everyday life. And it's then that I want you to be doing these exercises. I'm not asking you to go out there on a mission. I'm saying as part of your everyday life, build these things in, then they'll be natural.

And then, after we've asked for directions on Day 19 and we've had three days of practising that, we'll step it up again and ask for advice when we're in a shop. But we won't necessarily ask advice from someone who works there, maybe we'll ask advice from another shopper. And I'll be including some examples of what to say and how to do that in the lesson on Day 22.

Day 25 of the training, we step it up a little bit further, because this time we're actually going to ask for an opinion on something from someone. And, again, that will all be explained in that particular lesson.

Then, on Day 28, we really step it up and give you some great ideas of how to start a very simple basic conversation with a complete stranger in an everyday situation, where you'll be contributing and so will they. Maybe it's the library. Maybe it's the bus stop. Maybe it's the coffee shop. Maybe it's the bookshop, but you'll be aiming to a general conversation with somebody on Day 28.

And then, on Day 31, after you've had three days of practise in that, we'll do a recap.

So there you have it. That's the Zero to Hero Development Plan overview.

At any point during any lesson, if you've forgotten what it's about, simply come back and read this section again for a recap to get the context around what we're doing.

We're starting off really simple. We're overcoming the hesitation that you've got. And then we're starting to talk to people from a very, very safe place. And we're building on it with different situations every three days that get a little bit more advanced each time.

So go out there, have fun with it, and enjoy yourself!

Lesson 1 – Day 1

Welcome to your first training session. This is where it begins.

Imagine walking into a room full of people and feeling much calmer, relaxed and enjoying the event.

Imagine being out in public and feeling confident to strike up a conversation when you have something to say to someone, rather than pulling back and hesitating.

That is what talking with confidence is all about.

I have been there too – the hot sweats, the panic, the fear, the excuses to leave – and found a way to change it all; and I can help you too.

Over the coming week we will work on getting the hesitation level reduced, which then leads into the rest of the month focused on the plan. The Zero to Hero plan is designed to get you out there and talking to people in all different situations throughout the month, and beyond.

If you are stuck at any point, remember to refer back to the earlier chapters of the book for additional guidance in specific areas.

Today's training session

The first thing you need to understand is why you are not starting conversations and speaking to people.

Yes, we know it is fear, hesitation or feeling awkward. However, what causes you to feel that way?

The thoughts you are having about it.

When something happens and you think about saying something to someone, thoughts run through your mind, and then the hesitation and fear come up.

Therefore it probably isn't actually speaking to others that causes you fear but the *thoughts* you have about saying something to others. Think about that for a minute. It's a huge shift.

The thoughts that stop us are called limiting thoughts or limiting beliefs. In other words, you believe something about yourself and/or talking to others that limits your ability to do so.

Now, sometimes people know, or think they know, what these thoughts or beliefs are; sometimes they are right, and sometimes they may have other thoughts they're not aware of.

A lot of people, however, have no real idea of the beliefs or thoughts that might be holding them back.

That is why this first part of the plan is designed to get you discovering and understanding the thoughts and beliefs that are causing you issues. Once you understand what they are, you can start the process to change them.

You see, some people think about starting a conversation and think good thoughts and then do it; others think bad thoughts and don't do anything except hesitate and keep quiet.

I once thought bad thoughts about starting conversations with new people, but now I have nothing but good thoughts.

How did I change?

Well, that is what I am going to teach you through this course.

I've found that we can often easily summarize our issues or barriers in an "I can't" statement.

So, to easily describe their barrier or hesitation, many people will come out with one of these statements:

"I can't talk to people I don't know."
"I can't talk at parties."
"I can't talk when networking."
"I can't talk to strangers."

Which one of these "I can't" statements sounds most like you?

Is it one of them?

What would you more likely say?

What "I can't" statement summarizes you best?

Some people will jump on one of the above, many people will create their own.

Create your own if you can, your own statement that starts with "I can't" to describe your situation.

Make sure you have your "I can't" statement sorted for yourself before you read any further . . . dig deep and find the real statement that sounds right for you.

If you end up with more than one, that's fine; pick one to work through this process on, perhaps the most meaningful one, and you can always go back through the process with the others in future.

But make sure you complete the whole process over the coming lessons with just one of the statements, before starting on another "I can't" statement.

The reason is that very often when we change our belief about one statement, it can change the other statements anyway and they are no longer an issue.

Now, you have to realize that for most things in life where you say "I can't" it usually means "I won't because . . ." and what follows the "because" is some fear, imagined consequence or belief.

When you start looking at the "I can't" statement, there are some important questions you can ask yourself to start to break down that limiting belief.

With each of these questions and exercises over the coming training sessions, I urge you to not just think about it but write down as many ideas and thoughts that come to you for each question as you can. No matter how silly the thought might be, don't dismiss it because chances are it is affecting how you feel about talking with confidence on some level.

So, the first question – the question for today's training – is to ask yourself:

"How do I know I can't?"

This question is asking you to think about what makes you think you can't do this.

You see, we are often too quick to say we "can't" and believe it and not allow ourselves to break down what makes up that fear and gets us to declare the "I can't" statement to ourselves.

Usually what happens when people are asked "How do you know you can't?", is that they respond: "I just can't."

When we ask again and insist on an answer, they usually go to one of two positions:

1. "I've never done it" – which of course does not mean they can't.
2. "I did it once and it went badly" – well in this case it certainly does not mean they can't, it just means they did not get the result they hoped for.

Now, if you've attempted something and did not get the desired result, or you've never done something before, you need to understand that while you may need some skillset training, motivation or belief, it certainly doesn't mean you can't do it!

This is about realizing how things are possible for you, what would have to happen for them to be possible, and this is the first step – thinking about why you say you "can't". Because when you begin to understand it, then you can do something about it.

So all you need to do today is write down the answer to the question:

"How do you know you can't?" following the guide-lines above.

Tomorrow we will really get moving on this.

Lesson 2 – Day 2

Welcome to your second training session on talking with confidence, where you start to change and become a person who can talk and interact with other people no matter where you are.

If you've not yet done the previous session's exercise, go back and do that now and then come back to this lesson.

Now, as long as you've done the exercise from the last training session, you can move on to examine your "I can't" belief a bit further.

We explored looking at the evidence of why you say you can't do something through the question, "How do you know you can't?"

So now you are ready for the next step . . .

The next question to take this even further is to ask yourself and write down the answer(s):

"What specifically prevents me doing this?"

This starts your mind thinking about your fears, the consequences you imagine of what might happen if you did attempt it, and all the sorts of things you worry about that might or might not happen if you were to do this.

So once again, think about it and take your time, list on a piece of paper everything that comes to mind, no matter how insignificant it might seem.

List all the reasons and thoughts, the internal voice comments that come up when you ask "What specifically prevents me doing this?" – replacing of course the words "doing this" with whatever it is you are changing – for example, "What specifically prevents me talking to strangers" or, "What specifically prevents me from starting a conversation with people at a party?"

Take your time, think about it through the day if you need to, and you can keep adding to your list as ideas and thoughts come up.

In the next session, I will be helping you move things along even further.

First, you need awareness of what is going on and holding you back, then we can start to change it.

Lesson 3 – Day 3

So here we are again, I hope you are ready to really change things in your life in ways that will help you become happier, more confident and more successful, in life, business or your career.

So, in the previous session you asked yourself "What specifically prevents me doing this?" – and got all those fears, consequences and imagined outcomes written down.

Today is a little easier in that all I want you to do is think about this fear or limiting belief and the fact you "can't do it" and say to yourself:

"It's not that I can't do it, it's that I won't do it."

Do this several times throughout the day; start to convince yourself that, basically, it is under your control, you are the one who is deciding you can't.

Some teachings suggest you learn to think of something as being under your control by saying something like, "I can engage in the act of not . . ." followed by the activity or thing you fear doing.

For example "I can engage in the act of not speaking to people I do not know" or "I decide not to speak to people I do not know".

This may sound weird, but you will notice that the internal feeling or tug associated with this statement is a little (or a lot) different to how it feels when you simply say "I can't . . ." whatever your statement is.

So once again, think about it, ponder on it, and write your thoughts and answers down.

A quick recap of what we have done in these lessons so far:

I have asked for the evidence that causes you to say you can't do something by asking yourself:

"How do I know I can't do this?"

We then looked at the fears and consequences you currently associate with doing the thing you fear by asking:

"What specifically prevents me?"

Then we moved on to you understanding that you are **deciding** you "can't" and that this is under your control; and realizing it's usually that you "won't" do things as opposed to you "can't".

We are laying the foundations here to build on in the next lesson.

Lesson 4 – Day 4

You are doing these initial lessons and exercises on a daily basis at the moment, but soon we will have three days between lessons to practise. So if you are falling behind a little, that is OK. Simply work at your own pace until you've completed the previous sessions. Then move on to the next one.

I want you to make a list of all the positive impacts on your life if you were able to do the thing you say you can't do – i.e. talk with confidence to people you do not know very well, or at all.

Remember: these are the positives. How would it make your life better if you could do this with ease?

For example, things like . . .

I'd be happier.
I'd have more friends.
I'd be more comfortable around others.
I'd enjoy parties.
I'd be more successful.
I'd have more opportunities.
I'd be able to realize my true potential.
I'd be able to do the things I want to do for my family.

It's important they're in your own words and you write them down.

As we're working through this, you are probably already starting to think about talking with confidence to people in a slightly different way.

So, you have now made a list of all the positive impacts to your life if you were to be able to do the thing you say you can't.

Keep that list with you, read it a number of times through the day and notice just how good things will be in the future. Imagine doing those things and feeling good.

That's all you have to do today.

Lesson 5 – Day 5

If you have done the exercises from the last lesson, you will have made a list of all the positive impacts on your life if you were to be able to do the thing you say you can't.

Now we are going to look at it from the other side.

Make a list of all the negative impacts on your life if you never overcome this.

Remember: these are the negatives of never overcoming this, so they might include:

I will continue to be uncomfortable in everyday situations.
I will always dread going to events.
I will continue to feel I am letting myself down.
I won't achieve my full potential and will regret it in the future.

I won't be able to do all the things I want for my family. I'll never know just how good my life could have been.

It's important again that they are in your own words and you write them down.

You see – with today's question and the previous lesson – most people already do this, but they do it the wrong way round. They come up with all the positives of **not** doing something, and the negatives of actually doing it, and that is how they motivate themselves away from overcoming the fear or issue. If they think about attending an event or party, they think of all the negatives if they go and the positives if they don't, so they talk themselves out of it. Really, deep down, they know they would be happier if they were able to do these things.

With this lesson and the previous one, you have analysed the positives to your life if you overcame the fear and the negatives to your life of never overcoming it.

In life, we either motivate ourselves towards good things or away from bad things.

What method we use is based on our own way of using our mind and the context of our life it relates to.

For example, let's say we have two people both in a situation of having less than ideal (for them) finances and both wanting to be very wealthy.

Now, one may motivate themselves to do something about it by thinking on a regular basis about how good it will feel when they are wealthy, what they would do and how life would be.

The other person may motivate themselves by thinking about getting away from the bad situation of what will happen if things don't improve – will they lose everything, what other people will think, etc.

The first person is motivated towards the positive; the second is motivated away from the negative.

We are going to use your lists from today's exercise and the previous one in the next coaching session to see how you are motivating yourself. This has been a game changer for many of my clients.

Lesson 6 – Day 6

Today we are going look at what has been a game changer for many of my clients, using what we have done so far.

In the last two lessons you have been looking at the positives of overcoming the fear, and negatives of not overcoming it.

Today, I want you to read the positive list and negative list and see which one makes you feel more driven to overcome the fear. Is it the thought of all the positives you'd gain, or is it the thought of all the negatives you'd avoid?

For many of you there will be a difference in how the two lists feel; a few people may find the lists feel the same and are equal in terms of the amount of motivation each list gives them.

When you know what list motivates you the most, I want you to start thinking about that list in your mind several times today and really get an understanding of how important it is for you to overcome this.

We will do anything in life if we have a good enough reason! You've now got a list of powerful reasons to crack this once and for all.

If you have equal drive and motivation from both lists, then I suggest that you go with the positive list.

Next, the real fun begins

Tomorrow is the last of your daily lessons and the day you start to get out there and talk to people.

Before that, though, a recap of what we have covered so far.

Let's do a summary of what we have done with our initial "I can't" situation and add some more thoughts to it.

You have been thinking about your fear or limiting belief in a different way, and rather than just saying and accepting you can't do something, you've been taking the time to realize just how much it would mean to you to overcome this.

With all the understanding and knowledge you have gained about your fear, the evidence and the consequences, I want you to really think about how good it will feel with this fear gone. How great life would be.

I want you to play pretend like a child again and make those pictures in your head of you actually doing what it was you once feared. How do you look? How do you move? Just see yourself doing it and feeling good about it.

If it helps, put on some music that puts you in a good mood. Music is a great mood changer, so when the music is underway and the good feelings are running, do your visualization again, seeing yourself doing what you want to do and associating those good feelings with it.

If you do this a few times a day, every day for a few weeks, you'll recode your brain to associate different feelings with what it is you want to do.

Some people will get there straight away or after a couple of days, for others it may take longer.

You are basically developing a new habit. We understand it takes 28–32 days to develop a habit. However, depending on the degree of fear you once had, and the positive emotions you can develop when doing the above visualization, you can rapidly reduce the time - right down to minutes in some cases.

Lesson 7 – Day 7

So here we are; day 7. The end of our first week.

What a great day this is, because this is the day you get out there and start to talk to someone totally new.

After today, the lessons are going to be three days apart, until we get to the end of the month of training, taking you from Zero to Hero: from talking to no one to talking to absolutely anyone.

So, today is all about getting out there and just engaging very briefly with someone we already *have to* talk to.

This is a safe environment.

It's when you're buying a coffee, paying for your car fuel, paying for your groceries or shopping, maybe a courier is delivering you a parcel or the postman is giving you something.

Somebody that you're already engaging with at some level and are sort of in a conversation with, but you typically just do the one or two word pleasantries.

"Yes", "please", "thank you", "great".

We're going to extend that a little today. When I say extend it, I mean say a little more. Maybe comment on the weather or something else happening at that point in time.

So, take three days of doing this in various situations before moving on to the next lesson.

I remember when I was making my own change in this area. I went to get petrol for the lawnmower in a two-gallon container. When the assistant told me the price for the petrol, I said, "I remember when it only cost that to fill my car up for the week".

Once you've extended some daily interactions that already happen, I then want you to make a list of all the other situations and scenarios where you could do this over the next three days. Anywhere you could practise this even more.

Just saying that passing comment to someone.

It doesn't have to engage them in conversation. It could just be a passing comment, but you're saying more than you would normally say and you've already made good progress. In fact, excellent progress.

Stepping it up a little next time, you are going to do your first communication with a complete stranger, but it is very easy . . .

Go and do these initial extended interactions for the next three days and then come back for the next lesson. Yes, we cover a lesson every three days now for the rest of the one month course – the three-day gap is to give you time to get some really good practice in on each of the steps and exercises. Experts become experts by practice and by doing more of what works and less of what doesn't work.

Lesson 8 – Day 10

I trust you had a great time with the previous lesson, once you got into it, and you've now started to say a little bit more to people than you would normally say when you see them in an everyday transaction such as buying fuel, getting groceries or buying something in a shop.

So what we're going to do now is we're going to step it up. Every time we have a lesson, which is every three days now until the end of the course, we are going to step it up a little to the next stage.

So, what you're going to do is talk to a complete stranger.

This is somebody that you don't know.

Now, don't panic.

Because you're going to do this in a really easy way. We're going to build this up very, very gradually.

This is going to be what I call the "in motion passing comment".

Again, we're not looking to engage anyone in a conversation.

We're not looking to talk to someone for any period of time.

It's just about a random, one-off, throwaway comment. For example, "A little windy today" or "It's busy in here" or "Oh, you don't see many dogs like that these days".

It's just a one-off, random passing comment. You're not expecting the other people to engage with you or answer you. Great if they do, but it is not necessary. It's just for you to practise.

Why do I call it the "in motion" comment?

Because you do it while you're walking and you say it to somebody who is probably walking in the opposite direction. You don't stop; you keep on walking.

So, what happens is, you're not at risk of ending up in a difficult situation, where there's a deadly silence and you don't know what to say next.

Just a random throwaway comment; and when you have said it, you're going to be out of there!

There are many different examples that you could use. Many different things that you could say.

Let's say it's a really windy day and there's someone coming the other way and they've got a hat on. You say, "Mind your hat doesn't blow off!" Just a random passing comment that you're going to say and be out of there; an "in motion" comment.

In three days' time, the next step will be similar to today's exercise – although you will discover how to do the interaction in a static situation. This is where you are not walking but are standing still and waiting for a response from the other person. Let the fun begin!

Three days of practising this, and then come back for the next lesson.

Lesson 9 – Day 13

I hope you've been practising the previous exercise over the last three days and you're ready to move onto the next one. If not, don't panic. Go back over previous lessons. Redo some of the work.

Another useful thing you can do is keep a journal. Keep a journal – on your phone, on your notepad, wherever works best for you – of all the mini interactions you've had. Even the people you just said one word to; the person that you acknowledged. Keep them all in a journal. Write the date and write what it was. You'll be amazed when you look back in a few weeks at all of the wins that you've had. The things you didn't previously do that you're now doing. It'll absolutely amaze you.

Now then, it is time for another exercise to get out there and do.

We are stepping it up again.

In the previous lesson, you spoke to a random stranger with an "in motion" passing comment. Remember, it was a passing comment as you were in motion, so they may have been walking the other way and as you passed each other you said something, so there was no potential awkward standstill or quiet moment.

What we're going to do today is similar to a passing or "in motion" comment, in that it doesn't necessarily need anyone to engage in a conversation with us - it could just be a comment that is acknowledged and left. But we're going to do it in a "static situation".

This is where you are standing still when speaking, so there's no easy option to run away, because you're going to be in that situation before your comment and during your comment and after your comment.

So, a great example: let's say you're waiting in line in a shop or you're waiting in line at the bank and you say something to somebody in front of you or behind you about the line. You might say, "You'd have thought they'd put more cashiers on at lunchtime, wouldn't you?" Or, "I'd love to find a time to come here when it's not so busy". You know, just a passing comment. It doesn't matter what it is.

Important – the key is you say something; it doesn't matter if you don't get a reply. There are many reasons why someone might not reply and NONE of them have to do with you – unless you look like an axe murderer of course!

If they don't respond, it could be that:

They didn't hear you.
They didn't think you were speaking to them.
They are very shy.
They don't speak the same language as you.
And many other reasons.

Get out and do it today. Practise similar things over the next three days before moving on to the next lesson. Have fun with it.

Lesson 10 – Day 16

So, you're really making progress now and stepping things up.

What we're going to do now is step it up again a little bit and you're going to ask someone for help. Just ask somebody today if they could tell you what time it is.

A random stranger in public.

We're going to ask them if they've got the time.

Why is this stepping it up? Well, it's stepping it up because by asking for the time, we're asking for help.

We're asking for something and we're looking for a reply.

This is just a little bit on from what we've done before, although we're going to flip it on its head. If you remember, with the passing comment, we started with the "in motion" comment, so that we weren't stuck in the situation.

Whereas with the next stage that we went onto, it was in a static situation where we were standing at a crossing or standing in a line in a shop.

So we did "in motion" first, and then we did static.

What we're going to do today is we're going to ask someone the time in a static situation first, because it's easier when you are looking for a response. By this, I mean the other person is already standing still and you stop too.

If they're standing, waiting outside a shop or at a bus stop, they're in a static situation, and you can say something like: "Excuse me, have you got the time please?" They're just going to look at their watch and tell you the time, or they're going to say, "No, I haven't" and you can simply say, "Thank you" and walk on.

That's what you're going to do first.

Once you've done that and you've got that going, then what you are going to do is ask someone in motion who is walking in the opposite direction. You see this is a stage on, because what they've got to do is to stop to answer you.

When practising this, leave a good period of time, say 10 minutes, before asking someone else, and don't be in the exact same place. It might seem odd if you stand outside a shop and ask everyone who goes in and out what the time is!

Again, practise over the next three days, before coming back to move onto the next lesson.

Lesson 11 – Day 19

Here we are again. Welcome back. I hope you've been out there, practising these things and seeing the progress that you're making on a daily basis, and are now starting to feel really good about the new you that is developing through this.

We're stepping it up again a little, so you'll have three days to practise this one too.

What you're going to do this time is you're going to ask for help from somebody again, but you're going to do it in a way that makes you seem a little bit more vulnerable. It's not an awkward situation at all, but it's just a little bit more vulnerable. Because what you're going to do is ask someone for directions.

We're going to ask someone static, and then we're going to move onto in motion, like we did before with asking about the time in the previous lesson.

Simply say, "Excuse me, could you tell me where the nearest library is?" Or if you're in Central London you may say to somebody, "Excuse me, do you know the way to Trafalgar Square?" or anything like that. Just simple direction requests.

Perhaps even "Excuse me, could you tell me where the nearest Starbucks or Costa Coffee is?" You know, a simple, basic, direction-oriented question, where you're asking someone for directions.

For some people this is a little bit different, as I say, because it exposes a little bit of vulnerability. It says, "I don't know something and I need your help". It's a little bit different to the "asking the time" situation.

Once you've got that nailed down, tomorrow or the next day, before the three days are up and you move to the next lesson, try this with an in motion person – someone coming in the opposite direction.

Look to grab their attention.

Say, "Excuse me, you don't know where there's a Costa Coffee or a Starbucks do you?" Or whatever it is that you're comfortable asking for when asking for directions in that situation.

Next time, we move on to starting to talk to someone by asking their advice. This would typically start to lead you into more of a conversation than the previous exercises we have done so far.

So, do three days of practise before moving onto the next lesson.

Lesson 12 – Day 22

I trust things are going really well for you now. You know what I'm going to say . . . We're going to step it up a bit again. Yep, that's what we're going to do.

What you're going to do now is you're going to go into a situation where you ask somebody for advice. We're going to ask somebody in a shop for advice. You can start off by asking people who work there, and maybe even step it up even further and ask someone who is also a customer.

For example, I see somebody is looking at the cookery books. I go over and say, "Excuse me, I need to get a present for my cousin who is really into cookery. You haven't seen anything suitable for a beginner have you?"

So, get out there, ask somebody for some simple, basic advice about a product or what they'd recommend or if they've used something before.

"Have you used this before? Is it any good?" Just ask some advice from someone.

The reason it's a step up is because it has to initiate a little bit more of a to and fro conversation between the two of you, even if they say a simple "No".

Remember, their response isn't important.

If you feel like someone's ignored you, they probably didn't hear you or didn't understand you, or they're very shy. It doesn't mean you're doing anything wrong. We're all human beings. We're on the same planet. We are built to connect and communicate. It's only our in-built fears and beliefs as we've grown up that have held us back. So, get out there and have some fun.

Next time, we get to ask someone for their opinion on something. A bit like the advice conversation we dealt with today. An opinion-type conversation can open up into something special though. In three days' time, come back and continue with the next lesson.

Lesson 13 – Day 25

Today we are again looking at going out and talking to somebody – a random stranger, somebody we do not know – and asking them for their opinion on something. It's similar to the previous lesson.

Ideally, they won't work in the place where you're practising. You could be out in a bookshop, coffee shop, the usual situations, waiting for a bus, anything like that.

Ideally, you're looking for a friendly, open person. They may be smiling. They might look like they would ordinarily have a bit of a spring in their step, but they're probably going to be static.

They may be waiting in a line somewhere, they may be standing somewhere or they may be sitting, drinking their coffee or something like that.

What you are going to do is ask their opinion on something.

It may be on something you're wearing, or it may be an opinion on the cakes there or the coffees or something else.

If you've got the right intention and the right attitude, people will answer you.

A simple opinion-based question that you can ask somebody and get their response back.

Have fun with it. Remember to practise it. Keep your journal.

Anytime you feel like you've got a little bit stuck, go back to one of the previous lessons.

It's nearly time to discover how to start more of an engaging conversation with someone you do not know, and how you can get the other person to engage more in your conversation.

In three days' time we will be learning this and putting it into action.

Lesson 14 – Day 28

It's a big day today because now we're going to look to engage someone in a proper conversation.

We're going to go out and look for somebody to talk to who looks friendly and approachable and we're going to ask them a question or make a statement that's not closed. What I mean by this is, it's not something that somebody can easily just say "yes" or "no" to. We're going to ask them a question that causes them to engage and respond.

For instance, let's say somebody is standing at a bus stop and they have got a guitar case. You could say to someone in that situation "Are you in a band?" (which would be a closed question). They're likely to just say "yes" or "no" unless they're really good at conversation, in which case they'd answer you and then explain something about the guitar case.

You need to avoid the risk of getting just the "yes" or "no" answer because then you have to say something else in order to get the other person into the conversation.

This is one of the biggest keys to getting started in communicating and talking to absolutely anyone. If you saw someone with a guitar case, you could say instead:

"What sort of band are you in?"

Now, we've assumed they're in a band. It doesn't matter if they're not because if they're in a band they'll go, "Oh I'm in this sort of band" and then you've got some information to ask them another question. They will say something about the type of band they're in and you could ask them where do they play or how many people are in the band and you could start that conversation going from that point.

What if they're not in a band? Well then they'll say, "I'm not in a band". Well, so what. You could then continue with:

> "Oh, really, because you really do look like the sort of person that would be in a band and I saw the guitar case there. So what's that all about?"

Then they can respond again.

Can you see how saying, "What sort of band are you in?" is very different from saying, "Are you in a band?"?

Making that assumption, it puts you out there and, yes, you may be wrong, but so what? They'll just correct you. After all, they're the one carrying around a guitar, so a simple question like that can work wonders. Perhaps if they say "No" you could continue with "Really, you look like you ought to be in a band. If you were in a band what sort of band would it be?"

A key thing when you start to have these little conversations is to spot their engagement. You know you've cracked it and you know you're onto something when they start to get engaged in the conversation.

How do you know they're engaged in the conversation?

They're answering you. They're starting to ask you questions. They may be nodding, smiling, making good eye contact. They might be leaning in a bit closer in your direction.

These are all little signs of engagement from someone in a conversation with you.

The next lesson is an important reminder and recap of what you have learnt so far.

So, come back to the next lesson in three days' time after you've practised and got comfortable with this lesson.

Lesson 15 – Day 31

So here we are. Well done. You're at the end of the initial course.

We've been through so much here. You started off looking at what causes you to hesitate, and went through some exercises to help with that.

You started practising talking to people that you already see on a daily basis, who work in a shop or something like that, and just worked on that passing throwaway comment.

You then moved on to talking to people in a static situation, people in motion, asking for help or advice and even getting someone's opinion on something.

You went through so many different stages and this culminated in the last lesson where you engaged someone in a conversation.

I hope that all went really well for you.

There are more resources available on all of these things in my first book, *Think Your Way to Success* (https://www.markrhodes.com/think-your-way-to-success/) which is all about skillset and mindset.

Maybe it can help you with anything else that needs unlocking for you.

I wish you well on your journey of enhancing your life with the most powerful skill and ability that we can adopt, the ability to be able to talk to absolutely anyone that we want to talk to, of course.

Blog Articles and YouTube

There are lots of videos available to watch on my Massively Improve YouTube Channel:

https://www.youtube.com/massively-improve

You can also read additional blog articles and get updates on being more confident at:

https://www.markrhodes.com/blog/

I wish you every success on your journey to releasing the real confident you, the "you" that you are meant to be.

Mark

Mark Rhodes
Email: mark@markrhodes.com
www.markrhodes.com
Twitter: @rhodes2success

Index

Printed and bound by CPI Group (UK) Ltd, Croydon, CR0 4YY